Soaring Into Heaven

A Challenge for Christian Senior Adults

Ron Bowen

Copyright © 2018 by Ron Bowen

All rights reserved solely by the author.

Printed in the United States of America

ISBN 9781983809521

Unless otherwise indicated Bible quotations are taken from The **New American Standard Version** of the Bible. Copyright © 1995 by The Lockman Foundation.

Contents

Introduction
ARE WE VALUABLE?
Chapter 1: How is Your Value Meter?
Chapter 2: We are Still Valuable to Others!
Chapter 3: We are Valuable to God!
ARE WE FRUITFUL?
Chapter 4: Love and Joy
Chapter 5: Peace and Patience
Chapter 6: Kindness
Chapter 7: Goodness and Faithfulness
Chapter 8: Gentleness and Self-Control
ARE WE USING OUR TIME WISELY?
Chapter 9: As Time is a Great Resource
Chapter 10: By Praying
Chapter 11: By Studying and Teaching the Bible
Chapter 12: By Serving Others
Chapter 13: By Witnessing
ARE WE HELPING THE YOUNGER?
Chapter 14: By Being a Good Example
Chapter 15: By Attacking the Culture
Chapter 16: By Personal Relationships
RISE UP! RISE UP!
Chapter 17: Conclusion

Introduction

Job 12:12 "Wisdom is with aged men, *with* long life is understanding."

All of us started our Christian lives by putting our faith in Jesus Christ as our Lord and Savior. Some did this at an early age, maybe we were raised in a Christian home and our parents were involved in helping us make this decision. Some others made this decision as teenagers or young adults. We walked the aisle at a church or went to a Billy Graham crusade. Others made this decision later in life, maybe in our 30's or 40's and wished we had made it sooner. We all started by faith but at different times and at different places. But the purpose of this book is not about when we started **but about how we finish!**

We have been told to "finish strong" and to "press on" which is good, but I think it is far greater than that. This should be the most productive time in our life for impacting the kingdom. It should be an encore of such proportions that all that God accomplished through us in our life to this point would only be a fraction of what He will do now. Just as Samson killed more Philistines in his death than he did in his whole life, God can use us in mighty ways.

That's the purpose of this book - **to wake us up**. Those of us who call ourselves Christians, who believe in the Lord, and who are in the later stages of our life, maybe over 55 or 65. We have served God for some time, we have seen Him work in and through us and now we think we have finished the work. I want to tell you **the work is not finished!** There is far more to do, and God is looking for men and women completely devoted to Him such that they want to give their all and to **Soar into Heaven** going full steam and not limping along. We may be limping physically but we should be soaring spiritually.

This country (USA) is quickly moving away from God. Our priorities are so misplaced, what is right is wrong and what is wrong is right. But I have come to **deeply** believe that we are God's solution to the present dilemma of our country and the church. We can sit back and say we are retired (what a terrible word) or we can stand up as a mighty army to battle the forces of evil we see destroying our families, our society, our country, and our church. So the purpose of this book is to wake us up and to encourage, prepare, and strategically point us to where and how we can engage in the battle. I think God has uniquely qualified us to make a difference in at least four ways.

- **Experience and wisdom:** God says wisdom comes with age and experience. Job 12:12 "Wisdom is with aged men, with long life is understanding."

We have seen so much change over the last 50-60 years, and most of it is not good. The decline of morality and integrity in our culture has not only impacted the country in which we live but also the church we attend. Everything is so upside down, we no longer look to the elderly for wisdom and insight but to the young. How often do you see on TV where an 8 year old is spouting wisdom? Do you ever see them interviewing an 80 year old for wisdom?

Our society is so distraught with the moral decline, the disregard of the law, and the fall of the family and no one knows why. They keep asking our sports figures, actors, and politicians. They don't ask us. We have seen our country and churches being destroyed and **we know why**. Our culture has forsaken God and we are paying the price.

They think that restricting pornography is inhibiting free speech, but restricting verbal attacks on our government is protecting our national security. They don't understand that the free access to pornography is the greater threat to our national security. We have seen the moral decline in the movies, TV, and internet. But our leaders don't understand why there is so much rape, alcoholism, and drugs on our college campuses. They put men and women together in all kinds of situations, give them access to pornography and wonder why sexual crimes occur. How crazy is that.

The moral decline of our culture has impacted our churches. Recently, a friend of mine who was an associate pastor confronted the senior pastor about his involvement in internet pornography. Needless to say this is becoming more common in our culture which has greatly impacted our churches and our youth. The younger generations are leaving the church in large numbers and the church keeps trying to keep them with a more culturally contemporary style and form of the worship service. Changes aren't necessarily wrong but there has to be a better way!

We are the only ones who can remember what it was like 50 years ago, when it was common for families to pray together. Over the years, how often have you seen someone making a bad decision and you know the future trouble they are bringing on themselves. But they are naïve, they lack experience. Experience is a good teacher. If you have lived a long life you have gained some measure of wisdom as Job said to his young friends. In addition, God has given us the knowledge of right and wrong.

- **Knowledge of right and wrong**: "For the Lord gives wisdom; from His mouth come knowledge and understanding; He stores up sound wisdom for the upright ..." (Proverbs 2:6)

Our knowledge of right and wrong comes from God. We might not be Bible scholars but over the years we have received instruction in right behavior from God's Word. Our culture for a large part has lost the knowledge of right and wrong that God gives through His Word. Because of that our society and culture claim the prerogative to determination what is right or wrong. This political correctness has overwhelmed us and God is seldom in the picture. While I can't say we always get it right, but because of the knowledge of God's Word we can get it right more often than our society does.

- **Senior adults are the most generous:** "For I testify that according to their ability, and beyond their ability, *they gave* of their own accord, (2 Corinthians 8:3)

Senior adults are the most generous of any age group. A 2005 US Bureau of Labor Statistics report showed that 65-74 year olds gave more per person to a church or religious organization than any other age group. This is true even though their income is less than all age groups from 25-64. They actually gave twice as much as the 25-34 age group. The 75+ age group gave the most as a percentage of their income. They gave more than twice as much as a percentage of their income than any age group below 55. We have a better understanding that we are really laying up treasures in heaven. I will talk about this more later in the book

- **There are a large number of senior Christian adults:** Ecclesiastes 4:9-10 "Two are better than one because they have a good return for their labor."

If we step up as individuals we can influence some who will listen to us but if we step up as a united group we can change the course of this country and the American church. By the year 2032 there will be about 72 million adults over age 65 in the USA (about 20% of the population). My estimate is that about 25 million in this group will call themselves committed Christians. That is a huge army that can impact this culture.

Because of what we remember and what we know God has instructed us to do, **we need to step up.**

To help us on this journey I have divided the book into four sections:

- Are We Valuable?
- Are We Fruitful?
- Are We Using Our Time Wisely?
- Are We Helping the Younger?

In the first section "Are We Valuable?" I talk about our wrong perceptions that we are no longer useful. Our society, church, and perhaps family for a large part no longer view us as valuable but research shows they are wrong, and certainly we know, but sometimes forget, that we are extremely valuable to God.

In the next section "Are We Fruitful?" I discuss how we are doing with regard to the fruit of the Spirit. Are we growing spiritually? Character and integrity are lost arts and we need to be the leaders here. We need to look at **who we are** before we look at **what we do**.

In the third section "Are We Using Our Time Wisely?" I discuss how we as senior adults typically use our time and how we should be using our time. At this stage in our life we think time is our enemy but this section will show you that time can be one of our greatest assets!

In the last section "Are We Helping the Younger?" I discuss our responsibility to the younger generations. How can we bridge the gap when our society and church seem to keep us separated? We can truly be a great help to them and we need to take this responsibility seriously.

As I have stated before I think this can be the greatest time in our life to be used of God. We can do all things through Christ who strengthens us. Although we view ourselves as weak, through Christ we are strong, and I hope this book will be a great resource to encourage you and to help us **Soar into Heaven** going **FULL STEAM!**

Philippians 1:21 "For to me, to live is Christ and to die is gain."

ARE WE VALUABLE?

Chapter 1

Do you feel valuable?

Psalm 71:9 "Do not cast me off in the day of old age; do not forsake me when my strength fails."

WHAT HAPPENED? You used to be valuable. Now it seems like that value you once had is nonexistent or at least has decreased significantly. The seemingly decreased value happened slowly over several years, but what exactly happened? I know there are probably many factors that contributed to your perception of yourself as less valuable, but for now I just want to mention a few. The first of which is your job.

JOB

You have worked all your adult life, and now you find yourself retired. Maybe your retirement was voluntary, and maybe it wasn't. I retired from IBM/Lockheed Martin in order to take a job on staff at a church. I had pursued a master's degree in Theology, and I thought the church position would be a perfect retirement job. Only three years after I accepted the position, the church leadership decided to restructure itself, and I was out of a job at age 58. We sold our house and rented a place while we built a small home in a 55 and older community, and I looked for work. I applied for other church jobs; however, my brief three-year tenure as an executive pastor was not enticing to potential employers. Since the church job search turned up empty, and companies usually do not hire new managers of my age, I returned to engineering. After nine months of searching, I found employment with a small engineering firm some former colleagues had started. Before I found a job, I started to play golf with the retired guys in the community. On one of those days, some of us were in the pro shop waiting for the rain to stop, but because of the downpour and wet conditions, the pros decided to close the course. As we turned to go, one of the other men with his head down and with a disappointed look on his face said, "What do I do now?" I thought, "Is this retirement?" If you can't golf, is your day empty and without meaning? Do retired people just sit around and watch TV or do some other meaningless activity? How sad is that? Immediately my value-meter dropped. I couldn't afford to retire yet, but retirement didn't seem very attractive any way. I still needed my job not only for income but also for my own self-worth, the perception of my personal value, to remain relatively high.

Unfortunately, not everyone has the luxury of choosing when they will retire. Often people are forced into retirement for one reason or another. Donna Ballman, an employment lawyer, explains "11 Sneaky Ways Companies Get Rid of Older Workers" in Deborah Jacobs's 2013 Forbes article of the same name. Ballman explains that companies often reduce the number of older workers directly using job elimination and layoffs either through reorganization or reduction. Other more indirect methods of encouraging retirement according to Ballman include convincing the worker he is "suddenly stupid" or incompetent, cutting job duties, cutting job hours, or excluding the employee from meetings. Using Ballman's research, Jacobs (2013) reiterates the concept that older workers are encouraged to feel less valuable to the company and will therefore retire voluntarily. Retirees naturally then could begin their retirement feeling utterly useless.

Our self-worth or perceived value can come from the fact that we get up every day and go to a job that we do well and that gives us a certain satisfaction, or our self-worth may come from the income that job provides. New retirees, whether retiring by choice or not, not only need to keep their self-esteem afloat, they also need to keep paying their bills. Maria Bruno, a senior investment strategist and financial planner for Vanguard, explains that suddenly, you've gone from having a regular income to having no paycheck, and you wonder what you will do now (Satran, 2013). When you retire suddenly, it means doing practically the reverse of normal financial planning, Bruno says. In careful life-stage-based plans, people consider far in advance how to fund their big life goals. In the case of a sudden, unforeseen retirement, it's more a matter of first figuring out how to survive without a salary.

In his 2013 article, "Boomers Forced to Retire Face Unexpected Challenges," Richard Satran lists a number of ways retirees survive financially, and they include tapping savings, selling assets, and borrowing money. Those in our community either work full or part-time in order to make ends meet. Once you discover your way that you will maintain your monetary value, you will need to learn how to keep your self-worth.

I was talking to a follow golfer in our community who owned his own company but thought it would be a good idea to sell it and retire. Now he spends his time socializing on the golf course. He clearly misses the influence and recognition he received while working. He is set financially, but he still needs that human interaction and personal value that he lost.

Retirement can be a value stealer. We think we have less or little value because we no longer have that job in which we found success and at times our identity. If your value meter was based largely on your job, it may be pretty low right now.

SOCIETY

In her 1988 article, "The Psychological Tasks of Old Age," Victoria Howard (then Fitch) said, "Elderly people are often asked to stay out of the way, not make waves, and not be a nuisance to those who are younger." Howard continues in her 1988 work to explain the four tasks as she learned them through her experience with elderly people and her dissertation research: slowing, life review, transmission, and letting go. When Howard wrote that article, she was merely 42 years old and had so much more to learn. At the age of 68, Howard revisited her text and her topic in her 2015 article, "Aging in an Enlightened Society." Howard (2015) discusses societal attitudes on aging from a first person perspective this time and explains that ageism is defined as "the explicit and implicit devaluing of old age" and that society can contribute to that devaluing.

The common assumption is that the older people are a drain on society. They require medical care and are not productive members. Des Wilson in his United Kingdom article from the Daily Mail published May 17, 2014 stated, "We are told that the increase in the numbers of Oldies is placing an unfair burden on the young, who will pay for Oldies' care and pensions at a time when they themselves are battling to find work and homes." Wilson (2014) further explained that according to his sources, the elderly people in the United Kingdom were "applying massive pressure on our health and welfare resources making the [National Health Service] unsustainable." Throughout the article Wilson (2014) breaks down the negative arguments against the "Oldies" and debunks the argument that the elderly are society's pariah, but that does not change the underlying perception.

Other countries around the world have been facing similar issues concerning care for the elderly. Taro Aso, Japan's finance minister in 2013 suggested that the elderly are a drain on the country's finances. In a meeting of the national council on social security reforms he stated, "Heaven forbid if you are forced to live on when you want to die. I would wake up feeling increasingly bad knowing that [treatment] was all being paid for by the government. The problem won't be solved unless you let them hurry up and die." (McCurry, 2013)

Bioethicist Daniel Callahan (2013) wrote an often quoted New York Times article, "On Dying After Your Time" in which he emphatically states: "We may properly hope that scientific advances help ensure, with ever greater reliability, that young people manage to become old people. We are not, however, obliged to help the old become indefinitely older. Indeed, our duty may be just the reverse: to let death have its day."

If elderly people are taking the hint that society at large seems to disregard and discard them, no wonder they feel devalued.

FAMILY

Perhaps your value comes from your family. Social media is inundated with photos of families enjoying their lives: grandparents, moms, dads, kids. Happy people are smiling with their happy families living happy lives. Unfortunately, not all of them are as happy as they appear to be.

Families are struggling today mostly because marriages are failing. If your value was based on your marriage, and you are no longer married, your value meter is probably rather low. It is commonly claimed that half of all marriages in the United States eventually end in divorce, an estimate possibly based on the fact that in any given year, the number of marriages is about twice the number of divorces. Statistically this could probably have been your fate, and you endured a long, difficult divorce process. The natural feelings of failure following the ending of a marriage very likely added to a drop in your value meter.

Maybe your value was based on your children. At one time they esteemed you highly, but over the years, the relationships with them have become strained or non-existent. Perhaps this strained relationship is a result of your poor parenting methods. The perfect parent does not exist, and we all have failed to some degree, but maybe this hits you a little harder. All too often people who found their value in a job or career may have neglected their children. In today's environment, if there are two parents in the home they usually both have jobs to support the family's chosen lifestyle, and the children just didn't receive the love and attention they desired. A 1974 pop song written by Harry

Chapin, tells the story of a son who wants to spend time with his dad: "When you comin' home, dad, I don't know when, but we'll be together then, dad, you know we'll have a good time then." The story continues with the son going off to college and having a family of his own, and now the father is wanting time with his very busy son who just doesn't seem to value time with his "old man."

Perhaps you tried to live out your life through your kids. Maybe you never got to pursue the career you wanted, or maybe the dreams you had for yourself in your youth just never came true. Sometimes parents see themselves in their children and want to live vicariously through them. I could have very easily been one of those parents. All my childhood years, I wanted to be a professional baseball player, and I achieved some level of success at it. But during my freshman year at the University of Cincinnati, I had to decide between baseball and electrical engineering as a career. The engineering path was so intense that I simply couldn't do both. My logical mind picked engineering, which was the better choice for me and my family. Although I chose engineering as a profession, I never let go of my love of baseball, and I tried to achieve baseball success through my son Ryan. I coached him in two years of little league; Ryan was actually very good, but the league was not. This Little League organization was plagued with problems. I dealt with behind the scenes deals to get the good players, bad language and behavior by the coaches and parents, and even a racial incident against a boy I had on my team. Because of all that I felt God was telling me to give it up for the sake of my son, and we took him out of baseball.

If your relationships with your children or grandchildren are strained, they may be excluding you from family gatherings, which hurts our feelings and contributes to our already struggling feelings of personal value and self-worth. Your value meter may be dropping as you feel you no longer have the influence over your family that you once had.

CHURCH

Maybe you based your personal value on your church involvement. At one time you were highly involved and very influential, but now you have little input on the direction your church is going, and the only thing you are asked to do is to usher for the morning service. Youth culture has influenced the church, and most churches now target younger adults and families both for attendance as well as leadership. In a 2014 article titled "Keep Older Adults in the Church" by Ed Lewis, executive director of CE National, explains the reason churches are geared to the younger adults. It is Lewis's opinion that more church services are focused on the younger generations for the following reasons:

- It is a youth-oriented world.
- Young adults and high school graduates are leaving the Church by the thousands.
- Jesus gave us an example and chose men who were young to be His disciples.
- Young people keep us thinking about the future.
- Young people usually want to bring fresh new ideas for reaching people for Christ
- If we fail to reach and disciple the next generation we will lose them and need to re-evangelize.
- Christianity is only one generation away from extinction

People think the future of the church is with the young.

Several years ago, I was riding in a car with my daughter Renee and her family. At that time her two children Kayla and Marcus were about 5 and 3 years old respectively. Renee being the forever teacher was teaching them what the word *future* meant. After she explained it, she then asked them about their futures. They each explained what they believed their future would hold. Then she asked them about my (they call me Papa) future. After some silence Marcus confidently stated, "Papa has already had his future." We all laughed and continued on with the conversation, but the point remained that according to my 3-year-old grandson, at 50-years old, my future was already behind me.

Lewis (2014) explains that he understands why churches focus on the youth of our society. "But here is what scares me," he exclaims, "**We are losing our older adults!**" He recently asked 10 respected older believers why they had difficulty with all the methods and changes in the church. He asked what the major struggle is for them in seeing all these changes in the church:

- Is it that the church is changing to reach younger adults? **NO**.
- Is it because they do not like the music? They may not find it their choice, but that is **not** the reason they struggle.
- Is it that the informal service is the issue? **NO**.
- Is it that the church has gone to small groups instead of Sunday night services in most places? **NO.**
- Is it that the preaching style has changed? **NO**.

Then what is it?

"They overwhelmingly stated that they struggle with the changes in the church because **they feel they are not needed...not included...overlooked...made to feel like they are 'in the way'**" (Lewis, 2014).

For me and possibly you as well, it seems at times when I make a suggestion or comment to my church leadership that the comments aren't valued. In this way I can relate to the feeling of being "in the way."

The church you love and have served in for several years can have negative influence on your personal value and send your value meter needle into the red.

MENTAL ABILITY

Maybe your value is based on your mental abilities. You used to be able to solve complex problems quickly in your head, and now it seems to take much longer.

Just recently we took a trip to visit our grandson in Savannah, Georgia. As we were getting into Georgia, it began to get dark, and I couldn't tell if my headlights were coming on. I turned them on manually, just to be safe. When I did, the light on my dashboard that always came on when my lights were on did not light. After a while I could tell that my lights were working properly, but the dashboard light no longer worked. When we returned home, I took my car into our local dealer/service department. I had owned the car for about one year, but when I bought it I purchased an extended warranty, so it was still covered.

After about 5 minutes at the dealer, the nice young girl (probably around 30 years old) who checked me in came and asked me to show her the problem. She said their technician said that there was no headlight indicator on my car, just a high bright indicator and a fog light indicator. What I thought was the headlight indicator was actually the fog light indicator. I had never touched the fog light control; so if the fog lights are turned on, they actually come on when the headlights come on, and the indicator then lights up. When I had the car in for some body work the week before, someone turned off the fog lights. I didn't realize that they had been always on.

Needless to say I felt rather stupid and proceeded to tell the girl that I really didn't have Alzheimer's. She then told me that she was recently riding in a car with her father, and he drove right through a solid red light. That made me feel a lot better. ☹ It **seems** as we get older, we have more mental lapses, and with these lapses our own internal value drops. I have always worked on my own cars, and I still change my own oil, but the needle on my value meter definitely dropped some with this experience.

The American Psychological Association web site provides the following information concerning mental changes in older adults: "Cognitive changes, which are associated with mental processes such as sensation and perception, memory, intelligence, language, thought, and problem-solving, occur among aging adults.

- Because it may take older adults more time to encode, store, and retrieve information, the rate at which new information is learned can be slower among aging adults, and older adults often have a greater need for repetition of new information. Although it may take older adults longer to input and retrieve new information, daily occupational and social functioning among those over age 65 is not impaired.
- Short-term memory shows substantial changes with age, while long-term memory shows less age-related decline.
- Most aspects of language ability remain strong, yet word-finding ability declines with age. Three-dimensional drawing similarly declines with age.
- Wisdom and creativity often continue to the very end of life.
- Overall prevalence of mental disorders in older adults is less than in any other age group, and general life satisfaction among older Americans is as good as, if not better, than any other age group."(www.apa.org/pi/aging/resources/guides/older)

The constant changes in technology, and the quick adjustment our grandkids make to adapt to it also seems to diminish our value. A recent TV commercial shows a bunch of kids in a garage starting a high technology business. In the commercial "grandpa" is on an old computer and single finger typing data into it. They then point out that he is an intern and needs to step it up! Because we are slower to adapt to change, the culture and sometimes the younger generations seem to consider us to be antiquated and no longer valuable.

PHYSICAL CHANGES

According to the website of the American Psychological Association, "A number of physical changes occur as adults reach age 65. The most common are listed below:

- Hearing impairment among older adults is often moderate or mild, yet it is widespread; 48 percent of men and 37 percent of women over age 75 experience hearing difficulties.
- Visual changes among aging adults include problems with reading speed, seeing in dim light, reading small print, and locating objects.
- The amount of time it takes to respond to features in the environment once they are detected is typically slower among older adults.
- The proportion of older adults needing assistance with everyday activities increases with age. Nine percent of those between ages 65 and 69 need personal assistance, while up to 50 percent of older Americans over 85 need assistance with everyday activities.
- The top five causes of death among older adults are heart disease, cancer, cerebrovascular disease (relating to the blood vessels that supply the brain), pneumonia and flu, and chronic

obstructive pulmonary disease."
(www.apa.org/pi/aging/resources/guides/older)

With the onslaught of physical changes it seems like our physical issues dominate our conversations with our peers. We talk about our ailments, surgeries, and sometimes the more major issues like cancer. Our diminishing physical bodies cause us to be more insecure. Our decreasing eyesight causes us to trip and just to bump into things more often, so we feel clumsy. Our hearing loss is a problem, and our conversations are sometimes like a Ping-Pong match where we miss the ball a lot.

Several years ago we went back to our home town of Butler, Pa. While we were there, we took my wife Carol's mother to visit her sister (Carol's aunt). As we sat in the background, and Carol's mother visited with her sister, their conversation went something like that Ping-Pong match. Carol's aunt was very hard of hearing and had some memory problems, so to us the conversation was kind of funny. At the beginning, Carol's mother said that we were here from Virginia and had brought her over to visit. Carol's aunt then inquired who this Virginia was who brought her. **It went downhill from there**. I was pretending to read the paper, so I could hide my responses behind it. I tried to keep the paper from shaking too badly, but I just couldn't stop laughing.

At this stage in life, I now seem to get injured doing those everyday tasks like getting dressed in the morning. We adjust to the changes and mostly live normal lives, but the physical changes sure do put that value-meter into the red, because we no longer can do the things we once did. Recently we moved from our home of 15 years into a condo. As we were packing, I told Carol the boxes that we put in the attic when we moved in sure got a lot heavier when we moved out. It must have been all that accumulated dust. ☺

GOD

Because of the normal changes in our lives we feel like the needle of our value-meter has dropped so far that we even identify with the Psalmist in chapter 71 and fear that God has sidelined us like many others have. He writes in Psalm 71:9 "Do not cast me off in the day of old age; do not forsake me when my strength fails." Like him, we plead the same with God.

THE DREAM

Shortly after writing this chapter I had a dream. I sometimes have strange dreams, and this one was no exception. I dreamed that I was older and needed a job. (This was true but that was the only thing in the dream that was true.) I interviewed with a small company of young adults and got the job. I was so desperate to get the job that I didn't even ask how much I would get paid. In the dream I went to work, and they gave me a desk, but I had nothing to do. I would attend meetings about things I didn't understand and tried to convince them I could be valuable to them in certain other areas, but I was unsuccessful. They kept moving my desk, and finally I couldn't find it. I searched high and low but no desk was to be found. Then I received my first pay check and opened it in front of the leadership to find that the check was for $0.00. They all laughed. I know it was a dream, but even in dreams you experience the emotions as though it was real. **I felt worthless**. I hope you have never felt this bad, but maybe there is some truth in it for you as well.

Don't be discouraged; in the next chapter we will get a clearer picture of our true value and not our perceived value.

ARE WE VALUABLE?

Chapter 2

We are still valuable to others!

Luke 12:6, 7 "Are not five sparrows sold for two cents? *Yet* not one of them is forgotten before God. Indeed, the very hairs of your head are all numbered. Do not fear; you are more **valuable** than many sparrows."

In the first chapter, we reviewed some things that may have caused some of us to lose the value we perceive in ourselves. If we take a little deeper look, I think we will be surprised at those perceptions.

JOB

Let's review that job we lost or were forced to leave. Because of this early retirement, some older adults were forced to get other jobs just to make ends meet. The employers who hired these older workers are finding out some amazing truths versus the myths that have been spread.

A 2013 AARP article titled "The Surprising Truth About Older Workers" addresses these myths:

> **Myth:** Older workers are more likely to be burned out and less productive than their younger colleagues.
>
> **Reality:** According to a 2009 report from the Sloan Center on Aging and Work, hiring managers gave older employees high marks for loyalty, reliability, and productivity.
>
> **Myth:** Older workers are less creative, slower mentally, and more expensive to employ.
>
> **Reality:** According to Peter Cappelli, a management professor at the Wharton School of business says that "older employees soundly thrash their younger

colleagues. Every aspect of job performance gets better as we age." He states "I thought the picture might be more mixed, but it isn't."

Myth: Older workers are unequipped to multitask and juggle the technological distractions of the modern office.

Reality: The loss of cognitive skills that enable us to switch between tasks can be delayed with exercise and training. (Reade, 2013)

To maintain these cognitive skills, we need to play more computer games like bridge and spades. At least that is what I tell my wife, Carol. ☺

The AARP article stated that older workers score high in leadership, detail-oriented tasks, organization, listening, writing skills, and problem solving (Reade, 2013). Undoubtedly, the greatest asset older workers bring is experience – their workplace wisdom. They have learned how to get along with people, solve problems without drama, and call for help when necessary. Respect and honor can come with old age. Proverbs 20:29: "The glory of young men is their strength, and the honor of old men is their gray hair."

Employers are slowly changing from assumed perceptions to reality with the abilities and productivity of older workers. **We increase in corporate value as we age.**

The Interns Over 40 blog post author of "Older workers are America's Most Valuable Assets!" reminds readers that older people are punctual and have pride in a job well done. They are honest, loyal, attentive, and detail-oriented. The seasoned, experienced workers typically have good communication skills, set good examples, and become mentors to the younger ones. (Edelman, 2014)

My job situation in chapter one resolved by my getting a job with a small company that was started by former IBM colleagues of mine. The job with them lasted a few years while they had work, but eventually I was truly retired. Carol went back to work at Prison Fellowship after she had been retired from there for a few years. At that time, she worked three days a week, and it kept us from digging too deep into our 401k. She loved her job and coworkers, and she appreciated the impact that PF has in the lives of prisoners. She is a hard worker and very productive and was highly appreciated by her Human Resources department. Having my wife working while I stayed home was difficult, especially for me, to adjust to since I had been the primary bread winner for all our married life. God has given us a good life balance, so while she worked, I used my time to study for my church and community Bible studies and occasionally golf. ☺ It worked well for us, and she was valued by her coworkers. Similarly, one of the men in my Tuesday night Bible study just retired from full time employment at the age of 80. We can get a job and be valued in the workplace even later in life.

SOCIETY

Growing old is tough! It takes courage to grow old; therefore, given the proper support, old people could work to help the next generation understand this thing we call life (Fitch, 1988).

David Brindle from the Guardian thinks that older people are an asset rather than a drain on society in the United Kingdom. Brindle states that volunteering and caring responsibilities show that older people are net contributors to the economy. Research by the Women's Royal Volunteer Service indicates that because of their volunteerism efforts people aged 65-plus contribute more than 40 billion pounds more to the UK economy than they received in state pensions. This number should continue to grow as the "baby boomers" continue to retire. (Brindle, 2011)

Those same UK retirees help society by giving help to their children and grandchildren. Over a third of UK grandparents provide practical household help, including shopping and household chores to their children while nearly half provide daily care as well as material needs to their grandchildren. They also care for their elderly parents. According to the Guardian, half of people aged 50-64 with surviving parents provide them with household tasks. (Brindle, 2011)

In our church's senior adult community, we have taken the help of the elderly to a higher level. We lead a church wide effort in providing church services to many assisted living facilities. We also do bible studies, play games, and have sing along activities during the week. The leaders of these facilities love to see our volunteers as they encourage and uplift the members.

In the USA, similar statistics reveal the same benefits to society. According to data from the Corporation for National and Community Service, 18.7 million older adults – more than a quarter of those 55 and older – contributed on average more than three billion hours of service in their communities per year. Older volunteers meet a wide range of community needs - helping seniors live independently in their homes, tutoring and mentoring at-risk youth, providing financial education and job training to veterans and their families, and helping communities recover from disasters. In fact, older adults who volunteer typically volunteer more hours in a year than other age groups. In addition to providing valuable services to individuals and communities, older volunteers are also living more active lives through their volunteering. A growing body of research shows an association between volunteering and mental and physical health benefits. In particular, older volunteers report lower mortality rates, lower rates of depression, fewer physical limitations, and higher levels of well-being.

FAMILY

Maybe you fall into one of the family pitfalls described in chapter one. Suddenly your parenting days are over, and you find yourself a grandparent. It really hit me one Christmas several years ago when our son and daughter were visiting us with their young children. While watching them play around the Christmas tree, I suddenly realized we **really** were the grandparents. Sometimes I am a little slow, but then I got the picture. It crept up on me, and then it hit hard. But if you, like me, made some mistakes as a parent, for some of us God gives a second chance with grandchildren. Here are some highlights about the importance of grandparents from an article by Jeff Anderson titled "Why Grandparents Matter More than Ever."

- Grandparents Make a Difference in their Grandchildren's Lives

    Involved grandparents can make a big difference in the lives of their grandchildren. More than half of grandparents see their grandchildren in person at least once a week. This time and care manifests itself in healthier happier grandchildren.

    Dr. Karl Pillemer of Cornell University wrote, "Research shows that as many as 9 out of 10 adult grandchildren feel their grandparents influenced their values and behaviors. Grandparents transmit to their grandchildren the values and norms of social order."

A recent AARP survey of grandparents confirms that grandparents are comfortable giving advice to their grandchildren. For example, 78% of grandparents say they have discussed values with their grandchildren. Grandparents can also have a special role teaching family history.

- More Children Have Grandparents

    As the life expectancy has grown, so have the number of grandparents. While in 1900, less than half of American adolescents had at least two living grandparents, that figure had grown to 90% in 1976.

    Today there are about 80 million American grandparents, which is more than a third of the adult population.

- Grandparents Have Spending Power

    Grandparents are an economic powerhouse. They control an astounding **75% of the wealth in the U.S...** A good deal of that spending power is put to towards grandchildren.

    A survey by MetLife showed grandparents spend an average of $1,700 on their grandchildren annually. That support is often used to help pay for childcare or housing for grandchildren.

    It also manifests itself as gifts. According to an AARP survey, the most common item for grandparents to buy their grandchildren is clothing, and second is books. Fun foods (candy and snacks) and toys were also popular gifts from grandparents.

- Grandparents Love their Role

    According to an AGA survey, 72% of grandparents "think being a grandparent is the single most important and satisfying thing in their life."

- Grandparents Have Valuable Experience

    When you think about it for a moment, who could better provide advice and help raising children than someone who has already done it successfully? Grandparents put their past parenting experience to use in their interactions with grandchildren.

    The AGA survey indicated 63% of grandparents "say they can do a better job caring for grandchildren than they did with their own children."

- Today's Grandparents are Active and Involved

    Today's typical grandparents don't just sit in rocking chairs with blankets on their laps; they're active. Reportedly, 43% of grandparents exercise or play sports.

The value you seemingly lost through parenting mistakes can be back on the rise through grandparenting. You really are important in their lives. Two years ago I had the awesome privilege of performing the wedding ceremony for my grandson. That was truly a life highlight. I pray that you can be extremely valuable in the lives of your grandchildren.

CHURCH

In chapter one, I quoted some older church members who felt "in the way." The feeling of not being valuable has kept us from volunteering or taking on significant roles that we could fill. Much of the responsibility lies with the church leadership not recognizing the asset they have in their older adults. I strongly believe that **the greatest untapped resource for the church in modern America is its senior adults.** The common thought is since we are not paid, we can't have a significant role. Only the paid staff members should have leadership roles. That certainly is not the picture that the Apostle Paul painted. The older should be teaching and leading the younger. If your church recognizes this resource, your local body of believers can truly could make quite an impact for the kingdom.

I started to move my church in this direction when I was an executive pastor of a fairly large church. Our staff pastor in charge of men's ministry had resigned and moved on to another church. Since my staff budget was tight, I enlisted the role of a volunteer to lead the ministry without a salary; however, I gave him a financial budget and a paid secretary. The ministry flourished, and he did a great job for much less cost to the church. If churches could adopt this view for senior adult roles, we could be much more effective. Many senior adults have the experience, biblical knowledge, maturity, and motivation to finish strong.

Ed Lewis (2014) gives several ideas for using older adults in significant roles. His final point is to "challenge older people to leadership...not just service. They can lead groups, teach classes, offer counsel to younger people in the church and mentor others...and teach people that as we age we need to learn to demonstrate MORE of the fruit of the Spirit." Ed concludes his article by telling the churches to love the older people and mobilize them for service. They want to be involved in helping to make a difference! If you honor them, let them be honored by allowing them to be seen in church. They are just as important as other believers.

You can be very valuable to your church if you are allowed. Pray for and seek opportunities to make an impact. Please don't have the attitude that you are retired and therefore no longer need to serve. You really are needed even if your church doesn't seem to recognize its need for you yet.

MENTAL ABILITY

Although we know we lose some cognitive function in old age, the loss is really not as detrimental to our overall abilities as commonly thought. The American Psychological Association study showed just that:

- Although it may take older adults longer to input and retrieve new information, daily occupational and social functioning among those over age 65 is not impaired.
- Short-term memory shows less age-related decline.
- Most aspects of language ability remain strong.
- Wisdom and creativity often continue to the very end of life.
- Overall prevalence of mental disorders in older adults is less than in any other age group, and general life satisfaction among older Americans is as good as, if not better, than any other age group. (www.apa.org)

Carol's mother loved to play board games, so during most of our visits with her we did just that. She especially liked Yahtzee and dominos, and she could do the math quickly in her head. While playing Yahtzee, she could quickly determine the best next roll and calculate the results. She not only did it for herself but for everyone else in the game. She played games regularly until she died at the age of 90.

Even though we lose some cognitive capability, our knowledge and experience overshadow any ability that we may have lost.

I just recently showed a DVD to my Tuesday night community men's Bible study group about education in America. It was titled "Four Centuries of Education" by David Barton. In this David gives examples of third grade math tests in the early 1800s. He shows how complex they were, and how they had to solve several of the problems in their heads without using a pencil and paper.

I think this is actually an advantage we have over the younger generations. We were taught to solve problems mentally, and they have too many devices that generate an answer, but the device eliminates the need to understand the problem conceptually.

I love my engineer grandson who now works for Gulfstream Aerospace Corporation. We just recently went down to visit him and his wife in Savannah, Georgia for a Gulfstream family day, and he gave us a tour of the facility. Since I had designed some avionic equipment such as heads up and other displays, I was very interested. He did a great job leading our tour. He and I at times have some mental mathematic competition at which I can still knock his socks off. ☺ So be encouraged, if we haven't been inflicted with a mental disorder, we can still be mentally sharp and continue to learn. There are many opportunities at local community colleges and on-line to sharpen our skills and learn new things.

PHYSICAL CHANGES

We cannot deny the physical changes that seem to drop the needle of our value-meter, but we can do much to minimize that impact.

- In spite of a decline in physical health, two-thirds of older adults who are not living in institutions (such as nursing homes) report their health to be good, very good, or excellent compared with others their age. What's important to remember about people over age 65 is that while many begin to experience some physical limitations, they learn to live with them and lead happy and productive lives.

I just recently lost my family Ping-Pong domination when last Christmas my son beat me 5 out of 6 games ☹, but at least I got some exercise! Physical exercise is important to minimize the impact of our decreasing physical ability. I still need to have a regular physical exercise program, but my golf helps. We have a great golf course in our 55+ community. It is a tough executive course (par 62), but is very easy to walk. I regularly walk and carry my clubs, and I will be 72 years old this year. It's also great when I sometimes get paired up with some younger guys (20 something) who can hit the ball a mile. We recently played a winter league match against another club, and in this league the pros can play. I was partnered with our pro against the other club and their pro, and I actually beat their pro, another young guy who hits the ball a mile. ☺ If you stay physically active, it can help you to stay mentally active. Our value is not dependent on our physical abilities even though we can be successful in certain areas.

Thomas W. Rowland, MD, in his text *The Athlete's Clock* (2011) states that it is now well recognized that those who are physically active, on the average, survive longer than those who live sedentary lives because regular exercise reduces common health risk factors (Human Kinetics). Exercise and diet are important if we do both in moderation. Just remember that our value is not dependent on our physical abilities... even though it feels good to beat those younger guys sometimes. ☺

GOD

We are most importantly valuable to God. Our sense that God is finished with us is completely incorrect. We certainly remember how God used men and women in the Bible at a ripe old age, and God can do the same with us. This final point is so vital that I want to dedicate an entire chapter to it. So please join me in the next chapter to see how our God and Savior want to use us to impact the kingdom.

We are truly valuable to our employers, our society, our family, and our church. We need to realize our true value and let it motivate us to impact lives and our culture until God takes us home.

Ecclesiastes 4:12 (ESV) "And though a man might prevail against one who is alone, two will withstand him—a threefold cord is not quickly broken."

ARE WE VALUABLE?

Chapter 3

We are valuable to God!

2 Chronicles 16:9a "For the eyes of the LORD move to and fro throughout the earth that He may strongly support those whose heart is completely His."

In chapter one, we looked at things or people that gave us the perception that we have little value. In chapter two, we found those perceptions to be without merit. Now in this chapter we are going to look at the greatest assessment of our value. What does God think? Are we of value to Him or have we outlived our usefulness? I just want to look at two reasons why we are extremely valuable to God. The first is that we believe in Him. We have come to faith in Christ, and we will see how valuable a believer can be as an instrument in the hands of almighty God. The second is that we are **older**. Yes, you read that correctly. We are extremely valuable to God because of our age. We have not already had our future as my grandson said. God still has a future for us! Jeremiah 29:11 states, "[for] I know the plans that I have for you,' declares the LORD, 'plans for welfare and not for calamity to give you a future and a hope." So first let's look at our value as believers.

We are valuable to God because we have come to faith in Christ

We are valuable to God because we have come to believe in Jesus as our personal Savior. For me, I came to Christ at the age of 17. As a child, I don't think we went to church much until I was 12 years old. Then we attended a small country church. I can remember being in a boys Sunday school class and the teacher saying that good boys go to heaven and bad boys don't. I guess he was trying to get us to behave. ☺ My thoughts were, if that's true you have to be good all the time, every hour of every day, because you only live for a short time, and eternity lasts forever. I had a desire in me to know God and continued to question what I had heard. Later I found out that no one can be good enough to get to heaven, it's impossible. At the age of 17, I was dating Carol and attended her church on occasion. On one of those times I attended a Sunday evening service when the youth performed the service. Carol was in the choir, and I was sitting in the audience with her family. At the conclusion of the message by one of the youth, he asked for a recommitment for all the Christian youth and many went forward. Since this didn't apply to me, I stayed in my seat. He then gave an invitation to any who wanted to accept Christ for the first time, so I responded and joined the other teenagers at the front of the church. I then prayed to accept Jesus as my Lord and Savior. I could sense a weight being lifted off my shoulders, so I knew something significant had happened. That has been the single most important decision of my life, and I hope you have also put your faith in the one and only true God, Jesus. If you have, God views you as precious and extremely valuable.

We know we are valuable to God because of the huge sacrifice that He made for us. He left His exalted position in heaven where thousands of angels worship Him constantly. He came down to earth not as an angel but as a man. He experienced humanity for us and to the point where He suffered and died. He did that because we are valuable to Him and He loves us more than we can imagine.

Isaiah 43:4 states "Since you are precious in My sight, since you are honored and I love you, I will give other men in your place and other peoples in exchange for your life." He will give other men in our place and other peoples in exchange for our life." C.H. Spurgeon says that you are so valuable that "He will give all mankind for you..... whole nations of men for you." God will give it all just for you, because you are precious to Him. Spurgeon says "It is so wonderful that I should be precious to the All-Glorious Jehovah!..... I cannot believe it."

He says we are important to the world. We are like salt and light. We are so valuable to Him that He wants to use us to influence the world. Matthew 5:13a states "You are the salt of the earth" and Matthew 5:14a "You are the light of the world." Salt had two uses during that time, one as a preservative and the other as flavoring. God states that we help preserve the earth. How awesome is that! If all the believers were removed from the face of the earth the world would quickly spoil and go downhill much faster than it is going now. Salt was also a flavor enhancer. We as believers enhance the flavor of the world. The world is a much better place because we are in it. As believers we are valuable to God, and God wants to use us to impact the world.

We are valuable to God because we are older

We may feel like God has abandoned us, and we are no longer valuable to Him. Isaiah talks about how God will stay with the children of Israel, and I think that same principle applies to us today. Isaiah 46:3-4: "Listen to Me, O house of Jacob, and all the remnant of the house of Israel, you who have been borne by Me from birth and have been carried from the womb; even to your **old age** I will be the same, and even to your **graying years** I will bear you!" God will not abandon us but will stay with us just as he did with many of the Biblical figures like Abraham.

Abraham was 100 years old when God gave him a son through Sara. He lived to be 175 and died satisfied with life. Actually, most people don't realize that Abraham had another family after Sara died. Genesis 25:1 "Now Abraham took another wife, whose name was Keturah. She bore to him Zimran and Jokshan and Medan and Midian and Ishbak and Shuah." So even though he thought he was old when Isaac was born, God gave him another family, far past the point where he thought it was possible.

Moses was most used by God in the last 40 years of his life and died at the ripe old age of 120. He was still physically strong and was uniquely used by God. Deuteronomy 34:10: "Since that time no prophet has risen in Israel like Moses, whom the Lord knew face to face."

Caleb was 85 years old when he said to Joshua, Joshua 14:12 "Now then, give me this hill country about which the Lord spoke on that day, for you heard on that day that Anakim were there, with great fortified cities; perhaps the Lord will be with me, and I will drive them out as the Lord has spoken."

David also died at a good old age with honor. 1 Chronicles 29:28a "Then he died in a ripe old age, full of days, riches and honor;"

Job was also elderly, Job 42:17, "And Job died, an old man and full of days."

Our days also can be full up to the very end. I want to spend some time looking at some great encouraging verses from the book of Psalms.

Psalms 92: 12-15: "The righteous man will flourish like the palm tree, he will grow like a cedar in Lebanon. Planted in the house of the Lord, they will flourish in the courts of our God. **They will still yield fruit in old age**; they shall be full of sap and very green. To declare that the Lord is upright; He is my rock, and there is no unrighteousness in Him."

Please go back and read these verses again. There is so much there. The first thing that jumps out is the fact that the righteous man or woman can still yield fruit in his or her old age. God doesn't put us on the shelf for people to admire or forget. He wants us to be productive especially in our old age. I think this should be the most productive time of our lives. We have learned much through life's experiences, and God wants us to continue to bear fruit. Maybe we will even bear fruit in larger quantities than we ever did during our younger days. Retirement from the Christian life is not an option.

First the psalmist says, **"the righteous man will flourish like the palm tree."** He will flourish, grow, prosper, and thrive like the palm tree. This probably refers to the date palm because it was significant in the lives of the Jewish people. The date palm can bear fruit after 6-8 years and continue to produce fruit for up to 100 years. That's 92 years of productivity! God could do the same for us and give us 92 or more productive years. He doesn't want us to stop serving Him and impacting lives. Our value continues and grows throughout our aging years. This date palm has been and still is the daily food for millions. It was extremely valuable to the Jews. Its sap was used for wine. Fibers taken from the base of its leaves were used for ropes and rigging. Its stem was used as timber, and its leaves were used for brushes, mats, and baskets. The Syrians counted 360 different uses for the palm tree. (Smith's Bible Dictionary, 2000 Hendrickson Publishers)

God says we are valuable just like the palm tree. The palm tree was also used by the Jews as a symbol of victory and peace. That's why they covered the road with palm branches for the coming of the Messiah as Jesus entered Jerusalem. At this time, we can still experience victory and see how God can use us to defeat the enemy. How great is that! Also the palm tree is perpetually green. It doesn't turn brown or lose its leaves in the winter. It is forever green. The Amplified Bible translates Psalm 92:12: "We like the palm tree can be long-lived, stately, upright, and fruitful." (AMPLIFIED BIBLE, 1965, Zondervan)

Second, the psalmist states that this man or woman **will grow like a cedar in Lebanon**. The cedars of Mt. Lebanon are huge even though there are only about 11 groves remaining today. The largest grove has around 400 trees about a dozen of them are around 70 feet high and 60 feet wide. That's big! They are beautiful, durable, aromatic, and slow growing. They didn't get big overnight. It took time! We didn't grow strong overnight. We had to learn how to bend and depend on God. If we were stubborn and determined to go our own way, we suffered the consequences. Like the cedar, we can be strong in our old age. Actually some cedar trees have attained the age of 2,000 years reinforcing the theme of this group of verses that we can thrive in old age, even if we don't live to be 2,000. ☺ John MacArthur states that the cedars were objects of great admiration to the people of Old Testament times. Isaiah 2:13 states, "all the cedars of Lebanon that are lofty and lifted up." (MacArthur Study Bible, 2006, Thomas Nelson)

Third, he says if we are **"planted in the house of the Lord, we will flourish in the courts of our God."** What does it mean to be *planted* in the house of the Lord? It is my understanding that to be planted in the house of the Lord is to be born again. To begin to grow as a Christian we must first be planted in God's house. John MacArthur states, "A tree planted in the courtyard of the temple symbolized the thriving conditions of those who maintain a close relationship with the Lord". We must be planted, and we must stay close, maybe even as close as the branches are to the vine. ☺ If we are planted and stay close, we will flourish. The Hebrew word for flourish means to break forth as a bud, to bloom, to blossom, to grow, and to spring up. It also means to spread out as the extending of the wings to fly. We will flourish in the courts of our God. Nothing will be able to hold us back. We will bloom like the tree and fly like the eagle. Once we fly, we will see things from God's perspective, and we will understand. Proverbs 2:7: "We will discern the fear of the Lord and discover the knowledge of God."

Fourth, the psalmist states, **"They will still yield fruit in old age."** We will still yield fruit just like the date palm at 100 years old. The Bible includes many verses about bearing fruit. Colossians 1:10: "so that you will walk in a manner worthy of the Lord, to please Him in all respects, bearing fruit in every good work and increasing in the knowledge of God." We can bear fruit in good works and in the knowledge of God. The Bible shows three main ways we are to bear fruit: internally, externally, and through other people.

- Internally

We can bear fruit by allowing God to change who we are internally. Galatians 5:22,23a: "But the fruit of the Spirit is love, joy, peace, patience, kindness, goodness, faithfulness, gentleness, self-control." The internal changes occur because by the Holy Spirit is working in us.

- Externally

The internal change will impact our external actions. Hebrews 13:15: "Through Him then, let us continually offer up a sacrifice of praise to God, that is, the fruit of lips that give thanks to His name." What we say and what we do will be fruit.

- Through Other People

We will see changes in others around us because of the changes in us. This change in others is also a form of bearing fruit. Paul said in Romans 1:13, "I do not want you to be unaware, brethren, that often I have planned to come to you … so that I may obtain some fruit among you also." This fruit bearing is so important at this time in our lives that I have committed all of section two of this text to the Fruit of the Spirit.

Next the psalmist states **"They shall be full of sap and very green."** We will be full of sap. We will be strong. We will not be dried up spiritually and brittle easy to break and no longer bear fruit, and we will be strong. 2 Corinthians 4:16: "Therefore we do not lose heart, but though our outer man is decaying, yet our inner man is being renewed day by day." We should not be discouraged but encouraged. Our physical bodies may be getting weaker but our spiritual bodies are getting **stronger**. WOW! Does God use our physical bodies to impact the kingdom or our spiritual bodies? We could be the strongest we have ever been spiritually in this season of our lives. Then he says we will be very green. Not only will we be spiritually strong, but we will also be spiritually vibrant, active, and full of life! We may look old, but we are really young and energetic, spiritually speaking. ☺

> Psalms 92: 12-15: "The righteous man will flourish like the palm tree, he will grow like a cedar in Lebanon. Planted in the house of the Lord, they will flourish in the courts of our God. They will still yield fruit in old age; they shall be full of sap and very green. **To declare that the Lord is upright; He is my rock, and there is no unrighteousness in Him."**

The psalmist's conclusion is that the purpose of all this planting and growing and bearing fruit to old age is to glorify God by declaring His attributes to everyone but especially to the younger.

Psalm 71:18 (ESV) "So even to old age and grey hairs, O God, do not forsake me, until I proclaim your might to another generation, to all those to come."

This should be our theme verse. God give me the strength, energy, courage, and wisdom to proclaim your might to those who come behind me! Dear brothers and sisters, I firmly believe that the future of the church especially in America is with us, the older, not the younger. The church has had it backwards for several years now, and it is suffering for it. Our churches will soon be like the churches in Europe where they are being used as a museum or for skate boarding. The January 2, 2015 *Wall Street Journal* had a front-page article by Naftali Bendavid titled, "Europe's Empty Churches Go on Sale." The church attendance in Europe has dropped so drastically that the buildings are going on sale. Bendavid goes on to say that the closing of Europe's churches reflects the rapid weakening of the faith in Europe. The United States has avoided a similar wave of church closings for now because American Christians remain more religiously observant than Europeans, but religious researchers say the declining number of American churchgoers suggests the country could face the same problem in coming years. They are empty, and ours in America will be empty soon unless things change. (Bendavid, 2015)

Let me repeat what I said earlier, **the future of the church lies with the older not the younger.** I realize this is not politically correct, but I would like to give just two reasons why I believe this is true. First according to scripture, the role of the older is to teach the younger. I know that's not always the case, but generally speaking the older should be the teacher. We see many examples of this in scripture like David and Solomon and Elijah and Elisha. Second the growing magnitude of the senior adult population is staggering. The US Social Security Administration stated that the number of people over 65 has grown from 3.1 million in 1900, 4% of the total population, to 38 million in 2007, 13%. This number is expected increase to 72 million in the year 2032, 20% of the total population (Aging in the United States, 2012).

Just imagine what an army of this size could accomplish. Since we are losing the younger generations, the Christian demographic is aging, so this is even more critically important to the church. For this senior Christian army could truly be amazing we must set our priorities right. I'm not saying to abandon the younger but to use the older to guide, influence, encourage, help, support, and reach the younger.

ARE WE FRUITFUL?

Chapter 4

Love and Joy

Galatians 5:22,23a "But the fruit of the Spirit is love, joy, peace, patience, kindness, goodness, faithfulness, gentleness, self-control."

In chapter three, I mentioned that we will "still yield fruit in old age" and that I believe the Bible shows three ways that we are to bear fruit. The first is internal: those changes that the Holy Spirit performs in us which are taken from Galatians 5:22,23a,"But the fruit of the Spirit is **love, joy, peace, patience, kindness, goodness, faithfulness, gentleness, self-control.**" The second is external: how these changes impact the way we interact with people, and third is influential: how the changes in us influence changes in others.

First let's look at the fruit of the Spirit and how we are doing at letting the Spirit change us to be more like Christ and how those internal changes generally result in external actions. These internal changes determine who we are, our true character. As someone once said, "character is what you are in the dark." When no one else is watching, it's just us and God, what are we like?

LOVE

Scott Williams in a 2008 A *FamilyLife Today* article describes biblical love. The word for love doesn't refer to warm feelings but to a deliberate **attitude** of good will and devotion to others. Attitude is a little thing that makes a big difference. Attitude is a big deal, Charles R. Swindol states, (need source) "attitude is more important than the past, than education, than money, than circumstances, than what people do or say. It is more important than appearance, giftedness, or skill." It will determine how well we can impact others for Christ.

A loving attitude is fundamental as described in I Corinthians 13: "Love is patient, love is kind and is not jealous; love does not brag and is not arrogant, does not act unbecomingly; it does not seek its own, is not provoked, does not take into account a wrong suffered, does not rejoice in unrighteousness, but rejoices with the truth, bears all things, believes all things, hopes all things, endures all things." Jerry Bridges (2006) states that if you rephrase the virtues in love statements it might look like this:

- I am patient with you because I love you and want to forgive you.
- I am kind to you because I love you and want to help you.
- I do not envy your possessions or your gifts because I love you and want you to have the best.
- I do not boast about my attainments because I love you and want to hear about yours.
- I am not proud because I love you and want to esteem you before myself
- I am not rude because I love you and care about your feelings
- I am not self-seeking because I love you and want to meet your needs
- I am not easily angered by you because I love you and want to overlook your offences
- I do not keep a record of your wrongs because I love you and "love covers a multitude of sins" (I Peter 4:8)

Love is the foundation for all the other virtues listed. We can only love others because God first loved us. The first rephrase of Jerry Bridges (2006) from I Corinthians 13 talks about forgiveness. We need to be a forgiving people. At this stage in our lives, we can't have any hanging issues where we need to forgive someone.

I was about 3 or 4 years old when my parents got married. I was born out of wedlock, and my mother married someone other than my natural father. My mother's husband was the only father I ever knew, and he adopted me around the time I was 6 or 7. So from my earliest memory, he was my father. I did not understand that he was not my natural father until I was in college. I think he had a difficult time raising someone else's kid because my childhood was filled with turmoil. The earliest memory of my father was when I was turning 5 years old, and he was teaching me to tie my shoes. He would show me how to tie them, and then I would try it. When I tried and failed, he would slap me across the face until I was crying so much that I couldn't see my shoes. My mother apparently heard what was going on and came over and stopped him. As a result of this kind of behavior, I built up a deep hate and animosity toward my father.

I came to Christ at the age of 17, and somewhere around the age of 30, God just impressed on me that for me to grow spiritually, I had to forgive my father for all the problems around my childhood. I did that, and we had a good relationship from that time forward. I could still remember the wrongs he did to me as a child, but without any anger or bitterness. God removed it all!

You are probably wondering why I am telling you this story, but I think many others fall into this same situation. You probably have someone in your past you need to forgive, and I urge you strongly to do it even if the person is no longer alive. I think lack of forgiveness is a key contributor to our lack of love and continual struggle with bitterness.

In a 1993 survey by the National Council for the Elderly out of the United Kingdom, they stated that 50% of all young people viewed the elderly (over 65) as negative and cranky. I think this also applies to the USA. We are viewed as bitter and complaining. We complain about everything, all the time.

A couple of years ago we were vacationing in Florida and met up with some friends of ours for dinner. Our friends brought another couple with them so the six of us went to a local restaurant. The actual experience was horrific for our friends as the couple they brought complained about everything. They complained about the wait time to be seated and where we were seated. They complained about how long it took for the waiter to come to our table and how it took an eternity to get our food. Then they complained about the food and actually sent some back. It was a difficult time for our friends, and they apologized several times afterward. We just smiled and said to forget it, but it was truly embarrassing to think that's why waiters get anxious when they serve older people.

We, as a group, need to be recognized for our loving attitude so that we can have a positive influence on the younger generations. God says in Philippians 2:14 to do all things without grumbling or complaining. Yes that's right, **all things!** It seems like we can't do anything without complaining. We also need to understand that our complaining is not just toward others but also toward God. In Exodus 16:8b, Moses and Aaron, when dealing with the complaints of the Israelites said, "Your grumblings are not against us but against the Lord," and our grumbling and complaining is sin. Aaron recognized this when he was complaining about Moses. Aaron said to Moses in Numbers 12:11, "Oh, my lord, I beg you, do not account this sin to us (Aaron and Miriam), in which we have acted foolishly and in which we have sinned." God also dealt severely with the complaining of the Israelites. Numbers 11:1: "Now the people became like those who complain of adversity in the hearing of the LORD; and when the LORD heard *it*, His anger was kindled, and the fire of the LORD burned among them and consumed *some* of the outskirts of the camp." Many died as a result of their complaining. This is serious stuff!

We need to stop complaining and replace it with a loving, praiseful attitude. 1 Peter 4:9: "Be hospitable to one another without complaint." And John Calvin (need source) said "The more God has lengthened our days, the more we should be exercised in singing His praises." We can't completely change the younger generation's perception of the older, but maybe we can just one at a time. Be characterized by praise, and "Let no unwholesome word proceed from your mouth, but only such a word as is good for edification according to the need of the moment, so that it will give grace to those who hear," Ephesians 4:29.

We need to be loving to everyone. Matthew 5:43-44a: "You have heard that it was said, 'You shall love your neighbor and hate your enemy.' But I say to you, love your enemies and pray for those who persecute you. "We need to love our fellow believers. Peter says to "fervently love one another from the heart," 1 Peter 1:22b. I am amazed to see how police officers, those in the military, firemen, doctors, and nurses have a deep love for each other. They are in the battle to save lives, and because of that battle they have devotion and love for each other. Folks, we are in an even greater battle! We are battling for the souls of men not just their physical lives, but we don't have the same kind of love for each other as those I just mentioned. How sad is that! We have room for growth here, so let's remember who the enemy is and not be caught in the midst of friendly fire.

Think about the greatest act of love that you have personally witnessed or experienced.

Mark 12:30-31: "And you shall love the Lord your God with all your heart, and with all your soul, and with all your mind, and with all your strength. The second is this, you shall love your neighbor as yourself. There is no other commandment greater than these."

For me, I think it was my mother who in 1945 found herself pregnant and not married at the age of nineteen. During that time to be with child and not married was disgraceful, and she must have received a great deal of pressure to go away and have the child in secret and then give it up for adoption, but she didn't. She took the shame and raised me herself.

Mark 12:30-31: "And you shall love the Lord your God with all your heart, and with all your soul, and with all your mind, and with all your strength. The second is this, you shall love your neighbor as yourself. There is no other commandment greater than these."

Love is when the other person's happiness is more important than your own. - H. Jackson Brown, Jr. (goodreads)

JOY

In chapter 9, we will discuss how we can get more time, and one of those ways is staying in good health, but while good physical condition is one thing, we should also stay in good mental condition. Proverbs 17:22: "A joyful heart is good medicine, but a broken spirit dries up the bones." A joyful heart is good medicine for our physical well-being. We have all seen some people who were always upset about something and it seems like those people also struggle with many physical issues. I know we usually say that they are upset because of their physical struggles, and that could be a part of it, but maybe it's just the other way around. Their physical issues are a result of their heart (attitude) problems. In 1973, Dr. Grossarth-Maticek gave a brief test measuring habitual feelings of pleasure and well-being to thousands of elderly residents of Heidelberg, Germany. Twenty-one years later, he compared the test scores with health status. The results were amazing: **the 300 people who had scored highest turned out to be _thirty times_ more likely to be alive and well 21 years later than the 200 lowest!**

A study of 660 adults aged 50 and older from an Ohio community, published in the August issue of the *Journal of Personality and Social Psychology,* found that people who had positive attitudes about aging lived more than seven years longer than those with negative attitudes.

Jerry Bridges (2006) states, "The fact is only Christians have a reason to be joyful, but it is also a fact that every Christian should be joyful." The previous UK survey report (1993) stated that only 30% of the youth viewed senior adults as cheerful. I actually thought it would be worse than that, but it does get our attention.

We have so much to be joyful about! We should rejoice because

- God tells us we should rejoice:
    - Philippians 4:4 "Rejoice in the Lord always; again I will say, rejoice!"
    - Psalms 32:11 "Be glad in the LORD and rejoice, you righteous ones; and shout for joy, all you who are upright in heart."
    - Psalms 100:1 "Shout joyfully to the LORD, all the earth."
- God protects and provides for us
    - Ezra 6:22 "And they observed the Feast of Unleavened Bread seven days with joy, for the LORD had caused them to rejoice, and had turned the heart of the king of Assyria toward them to encourage them in the work of the house of God, the God of Israel."
    - Psalms 5:11 "But let all who take refuge in You be glad, Let them ever sing for joy; And may You shelter them, that those who love Your name may exult in You."
    - Psalms 4:7 "You have put gladness in my heart, More than when their grain and new wine abound."
- God has saved us:
    - Psalms 68:3 "But let the righteous be glad; let them exult before God; Yes, let them rejoice with gladness."
    - Psalms 71:23 "My lips will shout for joy when I sing praises to You; and my soul, which You have redeemed."

- - Luke 1:47 "And my spirit has rejoiced in God my Savior."
- We have a home in heaven:
  - Luke 6:23a "Be glad in that day and leap for joy, for behold, your reward is great in heaven."
  - Luke 10:20b "but rejoice that your names are recorded in heaven."

Most of the time we are discouraged and downhearted because of the struggles of this life.

> We live in a generally sad world, a fallen world well acquainted with despair, depression, disappointment, dissatisfaction, and a longing for lasting happiness that often never comes to pass. Moments of pleasure and satisfaction are scattered through the general pain and sorrow of life. Many people have little hope that their situation in life will ever change much, if any, for the better. Hopelessness tends to increase with age. Long years of life often become long years of sorrow, unfulfillment, loss of loved ones and friends, and often physical limitations and pain. Such decreasing times of happiness tend to produce a morbid sadness and lessening satisfaction with life. Most people define happiness as an attitude of satisfaction or delight based on positive circumstances

largely beyond their control. Happiness, therefore, cannot be planned or programmed, much less guaranteed. It is experienced only if and when circumstances are favorable. It is therefore elusive and uncertain. John Macarthur (2006)

As MacArthur stated there are some circumstances in our lives that tend to rob us of our joy.

- **Joy Robber – Other Christians**

One of those joy robbers is the behavior of other Christians. Paul stated in Philippians 1:15a, "Some to be sure, are preaching Christ even from envy and strife." And in verse 16 "they proclaim Christ out of selfish ambition rather than pure motives." If we focus on other Christians instead of Christ at times, we will be disappointed and discouraged because the best of men are men at best. Remember, we are all sinners and continue to fall short.

- **Joy Robber – The battle with the Flesh**

A second joy robber that we face is the constant battle with the flesh. Romans 7:15: "For what I am doing, I do not understand; for I am not practicing what I *would* like to *do*, but I am doing the very thing I hate." (italics added by NASB).This constant battle we are in is at times very discouraging. I often wonder if I can do anything without a selfish motivation.

- **Joy Robber – Loss of Loved Ones**

A third joy robber is the loss of loved ones and the fear of death. At this point in our lives, we have lost several loved ones to this life, and we know our turn will soon come. A great influence on the attitude of the elderly is the loss friends and relatives. This is very painful and can affect their desire to live. A while ago, I was watching a past television interview with Lucile Ball when she was in the later stages of her life. They asked her about her career and if she was still happy making people laugh? She shockingly responded that the joy was gone because all her friends she enjoyed working with are no longer here. She said, "It's no fun anymore."

- **Joy Robber – Physical Issues**

A fourth and final joy robber that we face is the battle with physical issues. Some of the typical things with people over 65 are:

- 40% have some hearing loss
- 50% have some arthritis or joint pain
- About half have evidence of heart disease
- Many have developed cataracts

In Ecclesiastes chapter 12, Solomon also gives some choice words on aging.

- The grinding ones stand idle because they are few - we lose our teeth
- Mighty men stoop - osteoporosis
- We look through widows that grow dim –cataracts
- We awake at the sound of a bird – have trouble sleeping
- Men are afraid of high places – lose our balance
- The almond tree blossoms – gray hair

In reference to losing our teeth, we do have something to be happy about. We are the first generation to keep our own teeth. ☺ Several years ago my grandmother was in the hospital and at the age of 97 was going through the last stages of life. She would sleep a lot and wake up for short times and would talk and then go right back to sleep. On one of those occasions, she must have been dreaming and she woke up and quickly asked us if we still had our teeth. Carol and I responded yes and she then said "great" and went back to sleep. So we can be thankful we still have our teeth. ☺

Living a long life is great, but we know that we will experience suffering at some point. God gives us some strange commands that we can't seem to grasp. He says we should have joy in suffering. Yes, that's right! James states in James 1:2, "Consider it all joy, my brethren, when you encounter various trials." Then Paul backs it up in 2Corinthians 7:4b, "I am overflowing with joy in all our affliction." What is that? Should we be glad that we are suffering because we enjoy the pain or the limitations? No, it's not the suffering itself but what God could be doing in and through it. Paul knew suffering. In 2 Corinthians 11:24 he stated, "Five times I received from the Jews thirty-nine lashes. Three times I was beaten with rods, once I was stoned; three times I was shipwrecked, a night and a day I have spent in the deep." In his later days, he was imprisoned in Rome, but even in his imprisonment he was joyful, not because he was in prison but because the gospel was going out as a result. He said in Philippians 1:12-14, "Now I want you to know, brethren, that my circumstances have turned out for the greater progress of the gospel, so that my imprisonment in the cause of Christ has become well known throughout the whole praetorian guard and to everyone else and that most of the brethren, trusting in the Lord because of my imprisonment, have far more courage to speak the word of God without fear."

One reason to rejoice in our suffering is that God could be using it for a greater purpose. A second reason to be joyful is that it's only going to last for a short time. Paul calls it momentary, in 2 Corinthians 4:17, "For momentary, light affliction is producing for us an eternal weight of glory far beyond all comparison," It's going to be short, God can be doing something great in and through it, and the end result is heaven!

In Luke chapter 10 Christ was telling the 70 not to be joyful because of the authority that Christ had given them and what they saw as a result, but rejoice in the fact that your home is in heaven. Luke 20:10 "Nevertheless do not rejoice in this, that the spirits are subject to you, but rejoice that your names are recorded in heaven."

My mother contracted ovarian cancer at an early age, in her late 40's. I watched as she went downhill from the cancer. I was in my late 20's at the time, and I had never shared my faith in Christ with anyone. Because of my love for my mother, I did share the gospel with her and found out that she had trusted in Christ at a church camp in her early teens. After that time, we would pray together, and often she wanted to talk about heaven. She knew that soon her suffering would be over, and she wanted to focus on what's next. The end of all our suffering is to spend eternity with our Lord. How great is that! So, when the suffering becomes too much to bear, **keep looking up,** and remember, heaven is the end result.

Think about a person in your life who was known for his or her joy.

For me one such person was a teenage friend, Bob Varnum. Bob was one of the most positive people I knew. He seemed to be happy and joyful all the time. He always called me "old buddy." We played basketball together, and he was instrumental in my salvation as we went to a winter church camp together. Bob wanted to go into the marines and then become a pastor. With such a great desire to serve God, I still don't understand why God took his life at age 17 when his car was hit by a train. Even now, I can still hear his voice and him calling me "old buddy."

3 John 1:4 "I have no greater joy than this, to hear of my children walking in the truth."

"Joy is the infallible sign of the presence of God." — Pierre Teilhard de Chardin

ARE WE FRUITFUL?

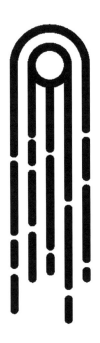

Chapter 5

Peace and Patience

Galatians 5:22,23a "But the fruit of the Spirit is love, joy, peace, patience, kindness, goodness, faithfulness, gentleness, self-control."

PEACE

As we strive to be godly men and women, one thing should be our overriding attribute – **PEACE.** "Peace is not the absence of turmoil, but the presence of tranquility even while in a place of chaos. It is a sense of wholesome and completeness that is content knowing that God controls the events of the day" (Williams, 2008). Peace should be the hallmark of our character. Jerry Bridges (2006) in his book *The Fruitful Life* gives three areas where we should be at peace. We should have

- Peace with God
- Peace within ourselves
- Peace with other people

Our peace with God comes from our salvation when we accept Christ as our personal Savior. We are no longer at enmity with God. Romans 5:1 states, "Therefore, having been justified by faith, we have peace with God through our Lord Jesus Christ." God is no longer our enemy but our Lord, Savior, Father, and Friend.

Next, we should be at peace within ourselves. Bridges (2006) states, "As Jesus finished talking to His disciples on the evening of His betrayal, He concluded with these words: 'I have told you these things, so that in Me you may have peace. In this world you will have trouble, but take heart! I have overcome the world.'

John 16:33." Christ said that we **will** have trouble, but He is in control. In my community, men's Bible study, we often discuss the world and American problems, and how everything is going crazy. After the discussion, we always remind ourselves that Christ is still in control. Because of that fact, we should have peace.

Finally, we should be at peace with other people. Proverbs 16:7b states "He (Christ) makes even his (our) enemies to be at peace with him (us)." That is a great promise from God, but I think we should also look at the first part of that verse. Proverbs 16:7a "When a man's ways are pleasing to the Lord." Okay, maybe that's why we have too many enemies; our ways are not pleasing to God.

Several years ago, I was a first line manager with IBM in a development engineering role. At that time, I was responsible for designing the fastest electronic device at that time for a competitive contract with the Department of Defense (DOD). We were under a lot of pressure to perform, and I was in constant conflict with the manager who had to build my design. God convicted me to go and apologize to him even though I thought he was totally at fault. I walked over to his office and went in and apologized. His response was not what I had expected. Instead of saying that he was also at fault and return my apology, he essentially said that I was right, **I was a jerk**. Even though he said that, after that time we became friends; the conflicts stopped, and we were at peace with other. We also completed the design and won the DOD competition.

We all want to be characterized as peaceful people, but at times we experience turmoil not peace. Some of that turmoil can be as a result of the physical changes we go through. As a side note about physical changes, Dr. Richard Alleyne (2008) stated, "Researchers have discovered that the older you get the more annoying you find background noise and how it becomes more distracting. The findings could explain why the elderly are less likely to enjoy loud music and parties than their younger counterparts." So, our dislike of loud music is not just because we still can hear, and we think the young people have gone prematurely deaf; but maybe it is actually for some other physiological reason. ☺

Seriously though, we can also be more prone to anxiety. Researchers don't all agree on this point, but Jeannette Franks PhD (2013), states in "Elderly Anxiety Disorders" from *aPlaceforMom*, "when anxiety becomes disruptive and disabling to a person's life, it is considered an unhealthy psychiatric disorder. As many as one quarter of all people experience anxiety to an unhealthy extent, and older people can be at particular risk. Seniors may experience more troublesome anxiety than other age groups for several reasons: they experience more losses, suffer from more pain and chronic conditions, are often on multiple medications that might exacerbate anxiety, and have confounding ailments." Franks lists some major types of anxiety disorders:

- **Acute stress disorder**: Anxiety and behavioral disturbances that develop within the first month after exposure to an extreme trauma.
- **Post-traumatic stress disorder (PTSD)**: Symptoms of acute stress disorder that persists for more than one month.
- **Panic attacks**: A sudden, unpredictable, intense, illogical fear and dread.
- **Social anxiety**: A preoccupation with how a person is viewed by others.
- **Generalized anxiety disorder (GAD)**: A pattern of excessive worrying over simple, everyday occurrences and events.

Hampton Roy, MD, and Charles Russell, PhD (2005) in the *Encyclopedia of the Elderly and Aging* said, "anxiety is common in the elderly with quite varying symptoms. Some people have nonspecific complaints such as apprehension, 'nerves,' or a feeling of going to pieces. Others complain of sweating, tremor, dry mouth, and blurring of vision. Anxiety is mostly a reaction to conditions of everyday existence such as personal loss, fear of dying, dependence on others, or perhaps the need to make a change in residence."

Have I made you nervous? ☺

About two years ago I went in for a normal check-up at my dermatologist. The check-up procedure went as others before it: he zapped some of the pre-cancer spots on my face that he blames on golf. Then he stopped and said that he needed to biopsy this one spot, and left the room. I think he went to get a sharp knife to cut into my face. As I sat there on the edge of the table waiting for him to return, I started to contemplate how this procedure of cutting a hole in my face would go down. I started to sweat and become light headed, and I thought I might pass out. I tried to adjust the table so I could lie down but I couldn't get it to operate. As I was debating what to do next a nurse came in, saw my condition, and quickly adjusted the table so I could lie down before I blacked out. This experience didn't help my manhood, but I could then relate to others with anxiety issues.

We can be anxious about a wide variety of different things, and certainly our health is one issue at the top of the list. Other areas of concern could be our finances, our children, and our grandchildren. So how are you doing here?

Anxiety can also be a joy robber as we discussed in chapter 4 because **we can't enjoy today if we are anxious about tomorrow.** Proverbs 12:25a: "Anxiety in a man's heart weighs it down." God commands us not to worry. Matthew 6:25 states, "For this reason I say to you, do not be worried about your life, *as to* what you will eat or what you will drink; nor for your body, *as to* what you will put on. Is not life more than food and the body more than clothing?" We are often told to give it to God, and this is good. 1 Peter 5:7: "casting all your anxiety on Him, because He cares for you." God cares for us, and that knowledge should be enough to calm our nerves, but often it isn't.

Sometimes our anxiety is a result of our sin, and we don't know what God is going to do about it. Is He going to forgive us and forget it, or is He going to discipline us in some manner? Psalms 38:18: "For I confess my iniquity; I am full of anxiety because of my sin." He gives us the solution to anxiety in Philippians 4:6: "Be anxious for nothing, but in everything by prayer and supplication with thanksgiving let your requests be made known to God." We certainly should pray about it, and if we have sinned, ask God to forgive us. The key part of that verse is to pray with **thanksgiving**. As we thank God for past provisions and protection, we remind ourselves that if God has watched over us in the past, He will certainly do it in the future. He is so interested in every aspect of our lives. He even knows the number of hairs on our heads. Matthew 10:30: "But the very hairs of your head are all numbered." How great is that!

Instead of being anxious, we should have an overriding attitude of gratitude. Hannah Whitall Smith said, "The soul who gives **thanks** can find comfort in everything, the soul who complains can find comfort in nothing." Our replacement for complaining is gratitude. God will continue to take care of us. When I was in college, God showed me His protective hand. I was in my third year of a five year program in electrical engineering at the University of Cincinnati. It was the first time I took Carol and Renee (our daughter) to Cincinnati with me when I went back to school after my co-op (work) session. I tried to plan financially, but I had a car accident, and I was so busy with school that I didn't realize we were running out of money. This was before charge cards, and if you ran out, you ran out. I could have asked for help from our families, but I was busy and didn't realize the situation. The day I realized we were broke I had two weeks of school remaining for the quarter. As best I can remember that very day we received money in the mail. This was the only time during school that we got any money in the mail. We received money from two different sources, Carol's aunt and my grandmother. They just said they thought we might need it even though we never said a word. As I thought about that incident over the years, I realized that God used the two people who were probably the spiritual leaders on both sides of our families. This incident has reminded me over the years that God is truly our provider. So we should not be anxious but be **thankful.**

Worrying is carrying tomorrow's load with today's strength. – Corrie tenBoom

God gives us peace through the working of the Holy Spirit, peace with our enemies, and peace with other believers. Paul challenges us in Ephesians 4:3. He states we should "be diligent to preserve the unity of the Spirit in the bond of peace," because Christ is our peace. Ephesians 2:14a: "For He (Christ) Himself is our peace."

Peace is not absence of conflict; it is the ability to handle conflict by peaceful means. - Ronald Reagan

Finally we should remember what the prophet Isaiah said "You (God) keep him in perfect peace whose mind is stayed on You, because he trusts in You." (Isaiah 26:3 ESV)

Patience

We have all said we won't pray for patience because God will send us trials. Trials are not something we desire, but they are a part of life. We, as older adults, sometimes get some unique trials because of our age. Jerry Bridges (2006) explains that the word patience, as we use it in everyday speech, actually stands for several different words in the New Testament, and it is used to describe a godly reaction to a variety of situations:

Patience – Suffering Mistreatment

Sometimes we will be mistreated because of our age: losing our job, not getting a promotion, or being denied medical treatment, for instance, but sometimes it can get ugly like this incident in Spokane Washington.

> SPOKANE, Wash. (AP) - Spokane police have arrested a woman who allegedly yelled at a slow-moving elderly couple and then pepper-sprayed the disabled wife in the face.
>
> Police say she apparently became upset when the elderly couple stopped their car outside a Home Depot store Sunday to wait for pedestrians and to let the 72-year-old disabled wife out of the car.
>
> Police say she yelled profanities at the couple and then pepper-sprayed the wife. Witnesses tried to stop the woman, but she got away.
>
> Police were able to track her down at home and arrested her for third degree assault. Firefighters treated the pepper spray victim and she was able to go home. (2012)

Hopefully you never get pepper-sprayed because you are old, but maybe you will have something similar happen to you.

Patience – Responding to Provocation

I know you are thinking that the woman in Spokane was an example of this, but I think she was being mistreated. Responding to provocation is more of an insult than physical abuse. These are actions of others that tend to arouse our anger and cause us to lose our temper. I will address anger when we discuss self-control, but it applies here as well. This may apply to someone who rejects our age as a position of respect, but we can choose to respond in anger or love. As I was researching this aspect, I came across an actual video on YouTube that someone captured that showed an elderly woman crossing the street. She was crossing at a crosswalk with a large purse or satchel in her hand. A convertible with a middle aged guy in sun glasses got impatient with her slow crossing and began to blow his horn. Not once but several times!! The elderly woman then hit the front of the guy's car with her purse, and the force was so strong that it tripped his air bag. Needless to say she got him back. She did lose her patience, but it was quite humorous and very fitting.

Patience – Tolerating Shortcomings

Matthew 7:5: "You hypocrite, first take the log out of your own eye, and then you will see clearly to take the speck out of your brother's eye."

It seems like at our age, the log in our own eye tends to grow quite a bit. ☺ Our whole world sometimes revolves around us. We focus on how others treat us and how incompetent they are. Remember the couple in the restaurant from chapter 4? They were impatient with everyone in the restaurant. At times, it seems like no one can do the job as well as we did or as well as they should.

1 Corinthians 4:7b (ESV), "If then you received it (from God), why do you boast as if you did not receive it (from God)?"

Several years ago, I was witnessing to a fellow coworker at IBM. He was an excellent engineer and a very smart man. It didn't take long for me to understand that he was a Christian and had accepted Christ as his Savior. But during our conversation, he stated that he no longer went to church. The reason he gave was people only went to churches that had good speakers for pastors. They only went to hear them speak. He thought that if God was in it, the poor speakers would have just as many people in attendance as the good ones. Needless to say, I was shocked at his intellectual analysis and didn't have an answer. This haunted me for several years until I understood the concept in 1 Corinthians 4:7. My coworker thought that the good speakers were self-made. He didn't realize that every ability we have comes from God. It is God who gives some the gift or ability to be good speakers. He was seeing God at work and didn't realize it.

In the same way, we should be gracious to those who are struggling. Sometimes they are doing the best they can, and we should first focus on the log in our own eye. Then graciously we can help others with issues or problems they might have.

Patience – Waiting on God

The next area that Bridges (2006) mentions in his book is waiting on God. It seems like no matter what it is; God's timetable is usually longer than ours. **It takes patience to wait.** In chapter 9, we will discuss time and how it is more of a benefit to us than a liability, but also for us it takes time to wait. Time is precious, valuable, and limited, and we think that God is wasting it. Oh, how short sighted we are! We only see today, but God can see what lies ahead. If only we could wait on Him.

There are several examples in the Bible of people who could not wait on God and suffered the consequences. Abraham and Sarah couldn't wait and as a result we are still experiencing the consequences today. Saul couldn't wait for Samuel, and as a result God took the kingdom from him. So, waiting on God is very important. Especially as we contemplate the difficult decisions we face, like when we should retire, if we have a choice.

Waiting on God is very difficult for me. I rationalize that if it's what God wants to do, now seems to be a good time. Since I can't see the future, my reasoning is flawed. Several years ago, I felt God wanted me in ministry and I was looking for an opportunity to make that happen. I had a good friend who was pastoring a small church in Florida, and I thought God **needed** me to go down there and help him. I worked out a temporary work assignment in Florida, thinking I would then retire and stay there on staff at his church. I had only one problem, my wife Carol didn't think it was a good idea. I forced her to go, and it was a disaster. We rented a place in a golf community halfway between my work location and my friend's church. We were about a 1 ½ hour drive to each location. As a result, we traveled up and down the west coast of Florida a lot. Through it God impressed on me that my priorities were messed up. I had put ministry ahead of my wife which was not a good idea. ☹ Once I confessed that to God, He almost immediately provided me a way of escape. About two weeks later, we were back in Virginia. Two years later, God did provide a ministry opportunity, and I was asked to come on staff at Reston Bible Church. So I am still learning to wait on God, but that was a life changing lesson for me.

Patience – Persevering Through Adversity

Bridges (2006) explains that we need to persevere through adversity. When you get to be our age, you have seen some adversity. Certainly some of us have seen much more than others, and this shouldn't be a surprise because Jesus said, "In the world you will have tribulation, but take courage; I have overcome the world" John 16:33b. My good friend Jamie Jackson has post-polio. He had polio at an early age but did not have any issues with it over the years until he turned 60 years old. Jamie went in for a normal spinal fusion operation, if there is such a thing, and after the surgery his polio kicked back in. Since that back surgery, he has had other back issues, weakness in his right leg, drop foot syndrome, hearing loss in both ears, and pain and nerve issues in his face and teeth. He is on many forms of medication which causes their own set of problems, and he has seen several specialists. His prognosis is incurable and it will continue to get worse and show up at various places in his body. Through it all, he has persevered, and God has used it in his life to focus him on ministry and helping others.

Patience is difficult, but we must trust completely on God knowing that all things do work together for good, Romans 8:28. We might not understand what God is doing, but we know it truly is for our good. God can sometimes do more through our waiting than He can do through our doing.

Patience is not simply the ability to wait - it's how we behave while we're waiting. - Joyce Meyer

Ephesians 4:2 "with all humility and gentleness, with patience, showing tolerance for one another in love."

Psalms 27:14 "Wait for the LORD; Be strong and let your heart take courage; Yes, wait for the LORD."

ARE WE FRUITFUL?

Chapter 6

Kindness

Galatians 5:22,23a "But the fruit of the Spirit is love, joy, peace, patience, kindness, goodness, faithfulness, gentleness, self-control."

KINDNESS

God wants us to be kind to each other with a forgiving attitude. He desires us to show kindness to everyone. Prov. 19:22a states, "What is desirable in a man is his kindness. " Micah says we need to embrace it. Micah 6:8: "He has told you, O man, what is good; and what does the Lord require of you but to do justice, to love **kindness**, and to walk humbly with your God." Above all we should be kind because of God's kindness to us. He showed the ultimate kindness to us by giving us the Lord Jesus Christ. Ephesians 2:7: "so that in the ages to come He might show the surpassing riches of His grace in **kindness** toward us in Christ Jesus." As a result of God's kindness, we can be saved. Titus 3:4,5a: "But when the **kindness** of God our Savior and *His* love for mankind appeared, He saved us." Kindness in Scripture can be an act of showing respect as the men of Jabesh-gilead did for Saul. 2 Samuel 2:5: "David sent messengers to the men of Jabesh-gilead, and said to them, "May you be blessed of the Lord because you have shown this **kindness** to Saul your lord, and have buried him.'" So the attitude of kindness should always result in a kind word or deed.

The definition of kindness is "a kind act or service." This act or service most often results in the generosity of the one giving kindness. David showed kindness by giving the land of Jonathan back to his son. In 2 Samuel 9:7 David said to him, "Do not fear, for I will surely show **kindness** to you for the sake of your father Jonathan, and will restore to you all the land of your grandfather Saul; and you shall eat at my table regularly." Our heart or attitude of kindness should result in acts of generosity just like Tabitha in Acts 9:36: "Now in Joppa there was a disciple named

Tabitha (which translated *in Greek* is called Dorcas); this woman was abounding with deeds of **kindness** and charity which she continually did."

KINDNESS – GENEROSITY

Acts of kindness often result in some form of generosity. We are the leaders here, but we can certainly step it up to a much higher level. The giving average percentage for the highest giving age group 65-74 is only 2.11% (after taxes) to church or religious organizations. This probably falls into the category of the rich giving out of their abundance rather than sacrificially. We need to continue to lead generously and to teach kindness and generosity to the younger generations just like the Proverbs 31 woman did. Proverbs 31:26 states, "She opens her mouth in wisdom, and the teaching of **kindness** is on her tongue."

We should be the kindest and most generous people on the face of the earth. Why aren't we? We certainly should be known for our kindness and generosity, but I think we fall a little short. We might look good in comparison to other age groups, but we certainly fall short when measured against God's measuring stick. If we would step it up here, the whole world would take notice, and Christ would be honored in a great and mighty way.

We are among the richest people on the planet. We don't realize how rich we are. If your household income is around $51,000 or your personal income around $40,000 per year you are in the top .57% of the world. Which means approximately one-half of one percent of the world has a yearly income greater than you do. (Poke, 2017)

We, as US residents, spend less on food as a percent of consumer expenditures than all the 83 countries the USDA tracks. We spend only 6.4% of all that we consume on food the remaining 93.6% is on goods and services. The food expenses as a percentage of income in other countries is much higher: UK – 8.2%, France – 13.2%, Japan – 14.2%, China – 25%, Russia – 28%, Pakistan – 40.9, Kenya – 46.7%, Nigeria – 56.4% (USDA, 2016).

We never think about whether we will miss our next meal or not, but usually whether we will eat in or out. Why don't we view ourselves as rich? I think we are so busy keeping up with the Joneses that we lose sight of how the rest of the world lives. When we read verses in the Bible about rich people, we think it is referring to someone else, someone who is richer than we are. If we acknowledge we are rich, then verses like those in James 5 are hard to swallow.

> James 5:1-6: "Come now, you rich, weep and howl for the miseries that are coming upon you. Your riches have rotted and your garments are moth-eaten. Your gold and silver have corroded, and their corrosion will be evidence against you and will eat your flesh like fire. You have laid up treasure in the last days. Behold, the wages of the laborers who mowed your fields, which you kept back by fraud, are crying out against you, and the cries of the harvesters have reached the ears of the Lord of hosts. You have lived on the earth in luxury and in self-indulgence. You have fattened your hearts in a day of slaughter...."

John MacArthur (2006) states that this refers to "Those with more than they need to live." James condemns them not for being wealthy, but for misusing their resources. These are the wicked wealthy who profess Christian faith and have associated themselves with the church, but whose real god is money."

Revelation 3:17: "Because you say, 'I am rich, and have become wealthy, and have need of nothing', and you do not know that you are wretched and miserable and poor and blind and naked."

Sometimes, we think God has blessed us financially because we are spiritual, and yet we may be bankrupt spiritually.

We need to acknowledge the fact that we are rich. There is nothing wrong with being rich. Some of the greatest biblical characters were rich, like Abraham and David for example. They primarily lived a life obedient to God, and they were rich. Our culture has misled us in this area, and that impacts our walk with Christ and our generosity. First, we must acknowledge that we are rich, and all the verses in the Bible that mention rich people apply to us, you and me. We are RICH!

We think we are self-made. We have worked most of our lives, and we think our accumulated wealth and possessions were accumulated because we are so smart or industrious. We don't understand that all that we are and all that we have comes from God. The Scriptures tell us we are stewards of God's stuff. These things are not ours, and we won't be able to keep them!

Because of being rich, there are detriments that keep us from being more generous. These are wrong attitudes that give us the desire to hold on to our riches and stuff. The first is the fact that inbred in our culture is a desire to be rich whether we consider ourselves rich or not.

Detriment 1 – The Desire to be Rich

This topic is full of controversy and a wide range of opinions. Some say the desire to be rich is good, and others say it is a form of mental illness. Those who say this desire is good will use Scripture to support their view and assert that the traditional Christian view is misled. Dwayne Gilbert, founder of wealthylifesecrets.com, states, "There is nothing wrong with wanting more out of life, including money. The man who does not desire more has something wrong with him and needs to seriously evaluate himself and his psychological wellbeing." He goes on to say that not wanting more to live a happier and more fulfilling life is a sin. He states that "Money is what allows us to live life to the fullest."

This cultural attitude goes way back. In an 1893 Baccalaureate sermon, the President of Brown University, E.B. Andrews spoke from the text of Matthew 25 (the one who hid his talent in the sand) about the benefits of making money and the necessity of wealth. He stated, "possibly your very best way to please God may be to make yourself as rich as you can become."

This desire to be rich has grown in our culture as a Christian virtue. We say that we want money so that we can give more to help others, but in truth it is primarily for our own selfish reasons of trying to gain happiness or security.

Ben Cohen (2012) states: "The desire to become rich is seen by some psychologists as a form of mental illness." He also states that "In modern society, we are conditioned from an early age to want things we don't need." In his article in *The Daily Banter*, Ben says that there has been found a direct connect between wealth and depression. He states, "The richer we are it seems, the sadder we become."

Because of the controversy in our culture, we desire to be rich, but we are not sure if it's a good or bad thing. A 2006 Gallup article entitled, "Most Americans do not have a Strong Desire to be Rich" states that only half (50%) of the people in their poll say making more money is a personal goal. I think because of the uncertainty about the good or bad of the desire to be rich, we won't admit it to ourselves or others. I can remember times in my life when I would be jealous of others with more money than I had. I think if we would admit it, we all could say that. What does God say on the matter?

Proverbs 23:4, 5: "Do not weary yourself to gain wealth, cease from your consideration *of it*. When you set your eyes on it, it is gone. For *wealth* certainly makes itself wings like an eagle that flies *toward* the heavens." Clearly the desire to be rich is not good, and it is a waste of time. We lose money as fast as we get it. Also, if we desire to be rich, we will be never satisfied with riches. Ecclesiastics 4:8b: "Indeed his eyes were not satisfied with riches." We all remember the famous quote from John D. Rockefeller, when asked the question, "How much money is enough?" He answered quite transparently, "Just a little bit more." Also in Ecclesiastics 5:10 Solomon states, "He who loves money will not be satisfied with money, nor he who loves abundance *with its* income."

I Timothy 6:9, 10 (ESV): "But those who desire to be rich fall into temptation, into a snare, into many senseless and harmful desires that plunge people into ruin and destruction. For the love of money is a root of all kinds of evils. It is through this craving that some have wandered away from the faith and pierced themselves with many pangs." Because of this desire some were limited in their generosity, and others have left the faith.

Think about some of your desires for things.

We just downsized from a house to a condo and were in the process of getting rid of large things and buying a few smaller things that would fit in our condo. My existing old desk would not fit very well, so we were in the process of looking for a replacement. The desks we found that would fit cost from $1,100 to $1,400 dollars. While we were looking, we stopped at a consignment store and found a desk that would fit perfectly in my den. But I had a problem with buying a used desk. It actually had some scratches on it! ☹ **WOAH** But God corrected my attitude about how I should spend His money, and we got the desk. I now have a great desk, and I am actually writing this paragraph on it. I spent only $499 for the desk, two file cabinets and a bookcase.

Being a good steward sometimes means buying a desk with scratches on it. ☺

Detriment 2 – We believe money is the source of happiness

We think money will bring happiness. To some extent this is initially true. If we are poor and struggle to meet basic needs, money can supply those needs. But if our needs are met, more money over and above those needs does not bring happiness. Proverbs 30:8b: "Give me neither poverty nor riches; feed me with the food that is my portion." Research has actually backed this up. Daniel Kahneman and Angrus Deaton of Princeton University found that happiness did not rise after a household reached an annual income of about $75,000 (Blackman, 2014).

Our culture tells us that to be happy we must have more money, and with that money we need to buy more stuff. In a 2014 study Professor Howell, associate professor of psychology at San Francisco State University, found that people think material purchases offer better value for their money than experiences. Even though those purchases only offer a temporary and short lived happiness. Thomas Gilovich a professor at Cornell University states "that new dress or the fancy new car provides a brief thrill, but we soon come to take it for granted." The research goes on to find that true happiness comes from giving our money away and by fostering appreciation and gratitude for what we have.

Professor Dunn (Walsh, 2008) has completed a series of studies in this and other countries and has found conclusively that "those who spent money on other people were happier than those who treated themselves." This was both with money that she gave them as well as their own money. A Gallup World Poll (SOURCE?) found that people who donated money to charity were happier, in poor and rich countries alike. Acts 20:35: "In everything I showed you that by working hard in this manner you must help the weak and remember the words of the Lord Jesus, that He Himself said,

'It is more blessed to give than to receive.'" People are happier when they give and not when they accumulate stuff. But we continue to gather stuff because we think it will bring us security.

Detriment 3 – We believe money brings security

Many have fallen into the pitfall of trying to get security from their money. Joe Gibbs said that bad investments and poor judgments cost him $1.2 million and left him virtually broke shortly after becoming head coach of the Redskins in 1981. At one point, he become so desperate that he said, "I got on my knees…. I said, 'Hey God, it's in your hands, I'm bankrupt. The only person who can straighten this mess out is You!" He said, "I was going to jump out and invest in this real estate boom and make enough money that I don't have to worry about things. I didn't put my security in the right things; I was trying to get it in money and other areas. I wasn't willing to trust God with my finances. I was looking elsewhere for security!" (Justice, 1991)

Our security is misplaced, and because of that our generosity is limited. 1 Timothy 6:17: "Instruct those who are rich in this present world not to be conceited or to fix their hope on the uncertainty of riches, but on God, who richly supplies us with all things to enjoy." We who are rich are warned not to place our security on money but on God. Our life does not consist of the stuff we have accumulated. Luke 12:15: "Then He said to them, "Beware, and be on your guard against every form of greed; for not *even* when one has an abundance does his life consist of his possessions." We may find temporary security in our things, but eventually that security will fail. Psalms 49:11-12: "Their inner thought is *that* their houses are forever *and* their dwelling places to all generations; they have called their lands after their own names. But man in *his* pomp will not endure; he is like the beasts that perish." We must fix our hope on God.

One of the ways to tell if you have a problem in this area is to evaluate how you handle losses, like a drop in the stock market or a loss of job. Several years ago, my son Ryan had just gotten his driving license. As he was driving by himself, a car stopped suddenly in front of him which caused him to bump into the car. Four construction workers got out of their car and walked back to look at the damage. They didn't see any damage and told Ryan to forget about it. I didn't think anything about it until I got a phone call from my insurance company about six months later. They asked me if Ryan had an accident on that day and said they were contacted with a claim for six months loss of work as well as significant hospital bills which totaled to several thousand dollars. They also said that since I didn't report the accident I was responsible to pay the claims. My first response was like I had been punched in my stomach. I thought I was going to lose my house and savings. My response was a clear indication that I was getting my security from my stuff and not God. After praying about it right then and there, God gave me a peace that I couldn't understand. A few days later after talking to my wife and Ryan, the insurance company said they believed our side of it and would pay the claim. Needless to say, I was greatly relieved, and I learned a lifelong lesson.

How do we be even more generous and truly "pay it forward?"

The concept of paying it forward has been around for a long time. The concept was described by Benjamin Franklin, in a letter to Benjamin Webb dated April 25, 1784:

> I do not pretend to give such a deed; I only lend it to you. When you meet with another honest Man in similar Distress, you must pay me by lending this Sum to him; enjoining him to discharge the Debt by a like operation, when he shall be able, and shall meet with another opportunity. I hope it may thus go thro' many hands, before it meets with a Knave that will stop its Progress.

> This is a trick of mine for doing a deal of good with a little money. (French, 2016)

The actual phrase may have may have been coined by Lily Hardy Hammond in her 1916 book *In the Garden of Delight*. She wrote, "You don't pay love back; you pay it forward." Ralph Waldo Emerson, in his 1841 essay *Compensation*, (SOURCE?) wrote: "In the order of nature we cannot render benefits to those from whom we receive them, or only seldom. But the benefit we receive must be rendered again, line for line, deed for deed, cent for cent, to somebody." An anonymous spokesman for Alcoholics Anonymous said in the *Christian Science Monitor* in 1944, "You can't pay anyone back for what has happened to you, so you try to find someone you can pay forward." On April 5, 2012, WBRZ-TV, the American Broadcasting Company affiliate for the city of Baton Rouge, Louisiana, did a story on The Newton Project, a 501(c) (3) outreach organization created to demonstrate that regardless of how big the problems of the world may seem, each person can make a difference simply by taking the time to show love, appreciation and kindness to the people around them. It is based on the classic **pay-it-forward** concept, but it demonstrates the impact of each act on the world by tracking each wristband with a unique ID number and quantifying the lives each has touched.

But is paying it forward a Biblical or a secular concept? Certainly, the idea of being generous is rooted in scripture. Ps 37:26a: "He is ever lending generously." Psalms 112:5a: "It is well with the man who deals generously and lends." But should our giving be indiscriminate or more selective? Giving indiscriminately is like going to the top of the Empire State Building and dumping out a huge box of $10 bills. I don't see this anywhere in Scripture. We should be wise in our generosity and know to whom we are giving. At least we should do our best in this area even though we can't always be sure.

As I am writing this chapter, we at the beginning of another presidential election, and the process of giving to someone's foundation to get something back is common practice. The Bible says we shouldn't give to the rich for the purpose of gain. Proverbs 22:16: "He who oppresses the poor to make more for himself, or who gives to the rich, will only come to poverty." We should give to the poor and give expecting nothing in return. Proverbs 21:13: "Whoever closes his ear to the cry of the poor will himself call out and not be answered." Proverbs 19:17a: "Whoever is generous to the poor lends to the Lord."

Be generous - Give to the poor

We have supported a Compassion International child for over 20 years. It is a great organization with a wonderful cause. I was also convicted by our pastor (Lon Solomon) who gives to the poor and homeless on a regular basis. I started carrying extra 5 dollar bills in my wallet to give when I see a need and opportunity. I know some are not honestly portraying their lot in life, but others are, and it's the ones that have a true need who I am trying to help.

Be generous - Give out of love

We need to give out of a heart of love. I Corinthians 13:3: "and if I give all my possessions to feed the poor, and if I deliver my body to be burned, but do not have love, it profits me nothing." Amy Carmichael said, "You can always give without loving, but you can never love without giving." If we don't love, we will not receive the benefits of giving.

Be generous – Give without expecting anything in return

We must give without any strings attached. The Bible says even to lend without expecting anything in return. Luke 6:35b: "do good, and lend, expecting nothing in return; and your reward will be great." We have done that a few times over the years. Our lending rules are to lend without any interest and the responsibility and timing of paying it back is between the borrower and God. The money will never come between us and our loved ones.

Be generous – We can receive eternal rewards

I think we have totally forgotten the Biblical truth that if we give correctly we can be setting aside treasures in heaven. We will be truly paying it forward. Luke 12:33: "Sell your possessions and give to charity; make yourselves money belts which do not wear out, an unfailing treasure in heaven, where no thief comes near nor moth destroys." We can and should give with eternity in mind. We should give to the work of God and to impact the kingdom rather than for our own selfish desires or the desires of our families.

Be generous and truly pay it **all the way** forward.

1 Timothy 6:17-19 "Instruct those who are rich in this present world not to be conceited or to fix their hope on the uncertainty of riches, but on God, who richly supplies us with all things to enjoy. *Instruct them* **to do good, to be rich in good works, to be generous and ready to share, storing up for themselves the treasure of a good foundation for the future, so that they may take hold of that which is life indeed."**

In all of human history, has there ever been a community of believers who has been given more than us? May what will be most important to us five minutes after we die become most important to us now. - Randy Alcorn

1 Timothy 6:6 "But godliness *actually* **is a means of great gain when accompanied by contentment."**

ARE WE FRUITFUL?

Chapter 7

Goodness and Faithfulness

Galatians 5:22,23a "But the fruit of the Spirit is love, joy, peace, patience, kindness, goodness, faithfulness, gentleness, self-control."

GOODNESS

Jerry Bridges (2006), in his book *The Fruitful Life,* states, "goodness is kindness in action – words and deeds…the Bible uses the word good to refer to what is upright, honorable, and noble about our ethical and moral character." We are in an integrity crises of the greatest proportion. That may sound overreaching, but I think it cannot be overstated. We are in an integrity free-fall that is destroying our country and the American church.

Integrity is the quality of being honest and having strong moral principles. True goodness reflects the character of God.

In an article titled "The Death of Integrity in America" Don Koening (2008) states, "at one time in America a man's word was his bond, most people had integrity. Today about one half of Americans simply cannot be trusted anymore." He states the root causes of the lack of integrity appear to be selfishness and having no empathy or love for others. It's all about ME. Our increased selfishness and greed certainly has much to do with it, but I think Chuck Colson (1993) hit it more accurately when he gave a speech entitled "Can we be good without God?" to Hillsdale College. We in America have pushed God to the back and wonder why crime has increased. We are trying to be good but without God's restraining influence. We have rejected the notion of absolute truth, and Colson (1993) states, "what we fail to realize, however, is that rejecting transcendental truth is tantamount to committing national suicide. A secular state cannot cultivate virtue." Without

God's restraining influence and without punishment appropriate for the crime, our criminals fear neither God or man. We don't understand how someone can go into a church, school, or theater and murder innocent people. Without the fear of God, what happens after they die, or without the fear of man, proper punishment that is a deterrent, they can do these abhorrent crimes. They don't care what happens to them. If the punishment hurts, it will deter the one who does the crime from doing it again. Proverbs 20:30a: "Stripes that wound scour away evil." If the punishment is severe, others will be deterred from doing the same crime. Deuteronomy 13:11: "Then all Israel will hear and be afraid, and will never again do such a wicked thing among you." Where we can, we need to bring God back and be in constant prayer for our nation.

The future of our country is dependent upon a return to integrity. If we can't get back to where we were, we will commit national suicide as Chuck Colson (1993) states. "A study conducted by Essex University on integrity suggests that an erosion of trust between people can have economic as well as social consequences. According to the report's author, Professor Paul Whiteley, an increase in dishonesty is usually accompanied by an economic downturn" (Evans, 2012). Even though this study is not done in the USA, I think the implications are the same. Again, I think we, senior Christian adults, are the key here!

An online study by the Michael Josephson (2013) revealed that lying and cheating is a growing problem. The problem is growing, and their study shows it is progressively worse from the older to the younger. In most questions about lying and cheating, the percentage of people willing to do it decreases with age. The study reports that the question "Do you believe one has to lie or cheat at least occasionally in order to succeed?" produced the following percentages of participants responded in the affirmative:

- Age 17 and under – 51%
- Age 18 – 24   - 36%
- Age 25 – 40   - 18%
- Age 41 – 50 - 11%
- Age 50 and over - 10%

I'm not sure if we are growing in integrity as we get older or that the culture is changing right before our eyes. Maybe it's a little bit of both. But even if we do get better when we get older, we are at the right place now to impact the younger generations. We have certainly seen many changes in our lifetime. On our television programs and in the movies, all the good guys lie. They constantly show that the end justifies the means. If you must lie to get a bad guy to confess or to give up information that's perfectly justifiable.

So why do we lie? It boils down to the shifting sands of the self and trying to look good both to ourselves and others. "It's tied in with self-esteem," says University of Massachusetts psychologist Robert Feldman. "We find that as soon as people feel that their self-esteem is threatened, they immediately begin to lie." For instance, in one experiment, Feldman put two strangers in a room together. They were videotaped while they conversed. Later, independently, each was asked to view the tape and identify anything they had said that was not entirely accurate. Rather than defining what counts as a lie and to avoid the moral tone of the word "lie," Feldman's experimenters simply asked subjects after the fact to identify anything they had said in the video that was "not entirely accurate." Initially, "Each subject said, 'Oh, I was entirely accurate,'" Feldman told *LiveScience*. Upon watching themselves on video, subjects were genuinely surprised to discover they had said something inaccurate. The lies ranged from pretending to like someone they actually disliked to falsely claiming to be the star of a rock band.

The study, published in the *Journal of Basic and Applied Psychology*, found that 60 percent of people had lied at least once during the 10-minute conversation, saying an average of 2.92 inaccurate things. **"People almost lie reflexively,"** Feldman says. "They don't think about it as part of their normal social discourse."

In a Gallup Poll taken from 1980 – 2014, people were asked to rate the honesty and ethical standards of people in different occupations. Nurses came in the highest and were rated at 80% of high or very high in their behavior. Telemarketers and car salesmen came in the lowest at 7%. Most occupations stayed flat over the 30-year period. Some increased slightly and some dropped but the most significant drop in all the occupations was with clergy. They went from 64% to 46% of a very high or high rating. Clergy are still rated higher than car salesmen ☺ but the drop is discouraging. Don Koening (2008) states, "there is a major problem in the lack of integrity in the clergy across denominational lines." We as senior Christian adults need to be especially concerned here and need to be a significant proponent of godly standards in this area. How can we impact a culture for Christ when Christian leaders are viewed as dishonest and unethical? James 5:12 states: "But above all, my brethren, do not swear, either by heaven or by earth or with any other oath; but your yes is to be yes, and your no, no, so that you may not fall under judgment."

How do we become integrity leaders?

Integrity needs to be important to us because it is important to God. The end does not justify the means because God is concerned about the means. If we focus on the means, God will take of the end.

- Integrity is shown through doing life.
- Integrity is taught through stories.

- Integrity is transferred through leadership.

Integrity is shown through doing life

As we go about our daily routine, we can show the importance of giving back even in small areas, when the cashier gives us too much change, for instance. Also, going back to the store when we realize we were undercharged or correcting a waiter when they left something off the bill. How about honestly reporting our income and paying all the taxes we should? These might seem like small things, but they are important because what we do in small areas we will also do in the larger ones.

Integrity is always an issue on the golf course and most everyone adjusts the rules slightly when they can get away with it. On one occasion, I was playing in an interclub match, and my ball came to rest on a cart path. If I took the correct drop (which you are required to do), I would end up under a tree limb without a shot. But the ball was close to being on the other side where I could freely drop away from the tree, besides my opponents were not around and who would know. I was tempted, but I took the correct drop and proceeded to hit the tree on my next shot. ☹ When we completed the hole, my opponent came over and complemented me on doing it correctly. He said most golfers would not have been that honest. People are watching even when you think no one can see. But most importantly, God is watching!

Integrity is taught through stories

Abe Lincoln was known for his integrity. One of his closest friends, Leonard Swett, said "He believed in the great laws of truth, the right discharge of duty, his accountability to God, the ultimate triumph of the right, and the overthrow of wrong."

One of the greatest stories I like about honest Abe was when he was offered a bribe. This version was told by Yury Tsukerman

(2010) who also said there is over 9,000 versions of it, so who knows which one is correct, but I like it anyway.

> When he was an Illinois attorney, Abe represented a poor widow who was suing the president of the local bank and asking for $5 in damages. The bank president, a pillar of his community, is alleged to have visited Lincoln's office and, in the presence of Lincoln's partner, offered Abe a bribe to throw the case. Lincoln is reported to have said, "No, the lady deserves her day in court." The banker responded that it would be humiliating if he lost to this widow, so he raised his bribe to $25. Lincoln refused. "$50," said the banker. Abe refused again. The banker stood up, started reaching for his wallet and said, "Mr. Lincoln, you drive a hard bargain. I'll give you $100 cash right now." Abe jumped up, physically grabbed the banker and threw him out the door, pitching him into the mud outside. Lincoln's partner was astonished, "Abe, he tried to bribe you three times and you didn't mind. Then the fourth time you just seemed to blow up," he said. Abe responded, **"He was getting too close to my price."**

Integrity is transferred through leadership

We live in a culture where influence comes mostly with authority. It is difficult but not impossible to influence someone without some sort of positional authority, but in a leadership role you can be more effective. This could come in the form of close friendship, but close friendships are fleeting. I think it most comes through some kind of leadership role. This could be leading a Bible study, golf association, community Board of Directors, community association, church group, business, or para-church organization. We look to those in leadership more than peers for guidance. Yes, I think this is still true even in the midst of a culture that attempts to undermine or degrade anyone in authority.

Think about those areas in which you presently have some kind of leadership role. Maybe you still have some influence over your children and maybe a little more over your grandchildren. Then think where you can take on a leadership role with a purpose in mind to transfer godly principles to those you lead. One of the things I do is to send out an email most every week to my family about something God has taught me that week.

Maybe you should take on a church leadership role. This could simply be teaching children. What a great opportunity to teach integrity to a generation that has lost its way because of lack of leadership. We can still be great leaders, and teaching and modeling integrity could be the most important thing we do.

Proverbs 20:7 states "A righteous man who walks in his integrity— How blessed are his sons after him.

"Integrity is keeping a commitment even after the circumstances have changed," - David Jeremiah

FAITHFULNESS

The Bible is full of examples about the faithfulness of God. Jerry Bridges (2006) states that God is faithful in many areas. "He is faithful for our final salvation, for deliverance from temptation, for the forgiveness of our sins, and for deliverance through times of suffering. Every aspect of the Christian life rests on the faithfulness of God."

When we think of faithfulness, we think of dependability, devoted, obedient, resolute, steadfast, trustworthy, enduring, and steady; where unfaithfulness is irresponsible, negligent, inconsistent, disloyal, and uncertain. We certainly want to be thought of as faithful because faithfulness is important to God.

Faithfulness is a direct reflection of our character. Luke 16:10: "He who is faithful in a very little thing is faithful also in much." Since our character doesn't change with the size of the task, the importance of being faithful in the small mundane daily things of life is extremely important. With faithfulness also come some benefits from God. Proverbs 28:20: "A faithful man will abound with blessings," Psalms 31:32: "The LORD preserves the faithful." God will bless and preserve those who are faithful to Him. But how are we doing in regard to faithfulness? Rick Warren (2013) says that God will evaluate our faithfulness in 7 ways:

- Do you possess the right values?
  A faithful person knows what's important in life and what isn't important in life. A faithful person knows how to invest his or her life. A faithful person makes their life count. A faithful person knows the significant apart from the trivial.
- Do you care for the interest of others?
  The second way God is going to judge our faithfulness is our relationship to other people. Did we care about the relationships of others and not just our own relationships? Faithfulness swims against the stream of contemporary culture, which says, "What's in it for me? What are my needs, my ambitions, my desires, my goals, my hurts, my values, my profit, my benefit? But God says faithfulness is proven by our others-directedness and by giving our life away, by looking at others rather than concentrating on ourselves.
- Do you live with integrity before an unbelieving world?
  In other words, a mark of faithfulness is the kind of testimony you have with unbelievers. We should be above reproach in the community and to have a good reputation, not only with believers, but with unbelievers. When God evaluates your faithfulness, He will be examining the way in which you walked before those who are outside the faith.
- Do you keep your promises?

When God evaluates your faithfulness, He's going to look at all the promises you made. Proverbs 20:25,"It is a trap to dedicate something rashly and only later consider your vow." It's easier to get into debt than to get out of debt - that's making a promise to pay. It's easier to get into a relationship than out of a relationship. It's easier to fill up your schedule than it is to fulfill your schedule. The Bible is saying that faithfulness is a matter of **if you say it, you do it**. You keep your promises. The number one cause of resentment is unfulfilled promises.

- Do you develop your God-given gifts?
There's a tremendous emphasis in the Bible on using the gifts and the talents God has given you. God has made an investment in your life and He expects a return on it.1 Peter 4:10 says, "Each should use whatever spiritual gift he has received to serve others faithfully, administering God's grace in its various forms. Notice it says if you don't use your spiritual gift, people are getting cheated. **Faithfulness is based on what we do with what we have.**
- Do you obey God's commands?
1 Samuel 2:35 God says,"I will raise up a faithful priest to serve me and do whatever I tell him to do." God defines faithfulness as obedience to the commands of Christ.
- Do you pass on what you learn?
The Bible talks a lot about the transferring process of multiplication. You're to give what you learn to faithful men and those faithful men are to give it to others, and so on. None of us would be here today if there hadn't been faithful men and women in the last 2000 years of the church. We're here today because some faithful men and women took time to write down the Scriptures, and others preserved the Scriptures, and others translated the Scriptures. We're here because of the testimony of faithful people. (Warren, 2013)

What are some areas in which we are doing ok?

Certainly one aspect of being faithful to God would result in being obedient by meeting together. Hebrews 10:25 states we should "not forsake our own assembling together." An ABC NEWS Poll (Sussman) stated that 38 percent of Americans say they go to religious services at least once a week. But there is a big difference across the age groups. The biggest gap is between the oldest and the youngest. Sixty percent of people age 65 and older report attending religious services at least once a week; where among the 18 to 30 year olds, just 28 percent go that often. Other ABC NEWS polls have found that religious beliefs and practices increase with age. So relatively speaking we are doing well in this area, but we are clearly losing the younger generations. They simply do not understand the importance of being in Christian community, **but we do!**

The same trend is found in having personal devotions. Senior Christian adults lead all other age groups in daily prayer and Bible reading. If we are truly the spiritual leaders, we need to step up and lead.

We are relatively faithful when it comes to generosity and integrity, but our faithfulness should not be measured on how we are doing with respect to the younger generations but how we are doing throughout our Christian lives? Are we standing by the stuff or are we falling away? Are we giving up or are we transitioning into heaven going full steam?

What are some areas where we are not doing ok?

As I am writing this chapter, we are planning to go to a memorial service this Sunday for a friend who this past week committed suicide. This past year has been hard for us in this area as Carol and I have known three Christians who took their own lives. Two out of those three were senior adults. They did not transition into heaven going full steam. We know they are now in heaven because of their faith in Christ, and that is very comforting to us and to their families, but the pain and impact to us and their Christian family runs deep.

Suicide is especially an issue for older adults. The suicide rates for people over 70 have increased dramatically in recent years. Some facts and statistics from the American Foundation for Suicide Prevention are:

- The suicide rate for men rises with age, most significantly after age 65.
- White men over 50 who make up less than a quarter of the population are responsible for almost 40% of all suicides
- The suicide rates for women peak between the ages of 45-64 years old, and do so again after age 75.

Risk factors for suicide among the elderly include the presence of mental illness – especially depression, social isolation, and physical illness. Over 60% of all people who die by suicide suffer from major depression.

Some suggestions on how we can help others who may be contemplating suicide (Hsu, 2013):

- If you see people who in depression, tell them, "Don't harm yourself! We are here for you."
- If you see any other warning signs get help and tell them about it. If needed, ask a pastor or counselor for help.

The number one cause of suicide is untreated depression. We need to help each other and to jump in when needed. We must also recognize that suicide survivors themselves face higher risks of suicide. If we face these trials ourselves, we need to be reminded that God can still use us greatly even in the midst of physical illness or loss of loved ones.

Another area where we are slipping is in regard to our commitment to marriage. We are starting to believe the politically correct verbiage that marriage is just a piece of paper. The U.S. Census Bureau data shows that adults older than 50 are among the fastest growing segment of unmarried couples in the U.S. They are living together but choose not to get married. Molly McCormack, a director of individual advisory services at TIAA-CREF, states "The biggest considerations couples have in deciding whether or not to remarry usually centers around their children and assets." She states, "If you're divorced and chose to remarry, you could lose alimony, pension, and Social Security benefits from your former spouse. If you're widowed, you could also lose survivor's pension benefits. Some couples may also want to make sure inheritances go to their children and don't get muddled."(Epperson, YEAR?)

Finally, we need to be faithful to the end. As I said before, we need to transition into heaven going full steam ahead and not limping along. We need to consider each day that God gives us as precious. Billy Graham (YEAR?) states in his book *The Journey*, "More than ever, I find, I see each day a gift from God – a gift I must not take for granted. It also is a time to reflect back on God's goodness over the years and an opportunity to assure others that God truly is faithful to His promises. Most of all, it's a time to rejoice in our hope of heaven." My good friend Patrick Arnone says that every day he lives is one day closer to heaven. How great is that!

1 Corinthians 4:2 "Moreover it is required in stewards that one be found faithful." (NKJV)

Think about a person in your life whom you would consider to be the most faithful.

For me I think it would be my mother-in-law, Carol's mother. Her husband was mostly gone before the birth of her last two children and then completely gone after that. She raised six children on her own by cleaning houses and working in retail. She always had the kids in church when the doors were open and was a good steward of all she was given. She truly was faithful to the end and died at the ripe old age of ninety.

Faithfulness is not doing something right once but doing something right over and over and over and over." - Joyce Meyer

ARE WE FRUITFUL?

Chapter 8

Gentleness and Self-Control

Galatians 5:22,23a "But the fruit of the Spirit is love, joy, peace, patience, kindness, goodness, faithfulness, **gentleness, self-control.**"

GENTLENESS

Jerry Bridges (2006) states that George Bethune in 1839 said, "perhaps no grace is less prayed for, or less cultivated than gentleness." Bridges (2006) also states, "Gentleness is careful never to be unfeeling for the rights of others. It recognizes that the human personality is valuable but fragile and must be handled with care." If we are gentle, others will be comfortable around us. We need to be sensitive to others' opinions and ideas, even if they are not scripturally sound. We need to listen and respond with sensitivity and respect. We truly need to esteem others higher than ourselves. Probably the biggest attribute of gentleness is humility. We need to be humble and then we can be gentle. Humility is truly the lost virtue.

HUMILITY – The Lost Virtue

In a recent Barna survey (2013) of Christian adults, participants were asked, "What's the most important quality in a leader?" Most respondents said integrity (64%) or authenticity (40%). One of the traits they were least likely to select was humility (7%). It's not recognized as important, but that has not always been the case. Kari Konkala (2005) asks the question "Have we lost humility?" He states, "Once regarded as the essential Christian virtue, humility has become to many 'a weakness or character flaw.'" Konkala (2005) did a survey of Christian literature from back in the 1600s up to today and found a tremendous difference in how the writers viewed the virtue of humility. He states that the writers in the late 1600s viewed that humility was the critical virtue. They examined in great detail the benefit of humility to the person as well as to society. It was even viewed as a sign of manliness: "A truly masculine, pious seventeenth-century Englishman was humble." Konkala (2005) states, "In the course of the last three centuries the central moral teaching concerning humility seems to have faded away so completely that entries for this virtue of Christ are not found in *The Encyclopedia of Religion*." He also states, "the survey of recent reference works of Christianity reveals a common trend: humility is passed over in total silence." What exactly is humility?

HUMILITY DEFINED

Andy Stanley states, "Humility involves seeing yourself accurately in relationship with others as a result of your relationship with God. Jesus followers are nothing more than citizens of humanity, just like everyone else. Every person is loved by God. That's the great equalizer that cuts through class, wealth, education, and talent. Jesus followers approach others as peers regardless of what they do or don't do, how much they have, or how much or little they've accomplished." The Christian Bible Reference Site states, "In the Bible, humility or humbleness is a quality of being courteously respectful of others. It is the opposite of aggressiveness, arrogance, boastfulness, and vanity. Rather than, 'Me first,' humility allows us to say, 'No, you first, my friend.' Humility is the quality that lets us go more than halfway to meet the needs and demands of others."

Philippians 2:3 "Do nothing from selfishness or empty conceit, but with humility of mind regard one another as more important than yourselves."

How do we communicate **me** first?

- General knowledge arrogance – As a young engineer, I found that a common battle between engineers was to see who was smarter. On one occasion I found myself in such a battle and proceeded to prove to the other engineer that I was truly smarter than he was. I won the battle but lost all future opportunities to share Christ with him. I still regret that action to this day.

- Bible knowledge arrogance – This battle is usually between Christians but not always. We think if we can show that we know more about the Bible then we are more spiritual that others. How wrong that is!
- Riches arrogance – We love to talk about our stuff. The size of our home, the kind of car we drive, or the vacation homes we have. If we have more stuff, then we must be more important.
- Position arrogance – We talk about our past or present positions of authority. When we first started attending McLean Bible Church's Manassas campus, a man who didn't know me very well thought all I talked about was my past position as an executive pastor at a church of 1,500 people. It took a few years to get over that initial set back in our relationship.

What do you think are the characteristics of a humble person? Certainly, a person who asks questions about you is humble. He values your input and has many counselors whom he relies on. He doesn't retaliate when offended.

You are driving down the interstate and the traffic is heavy. In the distance is a slow-moving truck in the right lane, and you are in a line in the left lane waiting to pass the truck. Suddenly a car passes you on the right and pulls in front of you almost hitting your car. How do you respond? Do you blow your horn, flash your lights, or stay right on their bumper? Maybe the better question is, do you do all three? OK, I admit sometimes I do as well. But the Bible says:

- Proverbs 24:29a – "Do not say, 'Thus I shall do to him as he has done to me;'"
- Proverbs 10:12b, - "But love covers all transgressions."
- Proverbs 19:11b - "And it is his glory to overlook a transgression"

A humble person is never defensive. When I was the executive pastor at RBC an outside consultant informed me that I was defensive when criticized by others. After my initial defensive response, ☺ I took it to heart and looked up and highlighted all the verses in Proverbs about handling reproof. They helped me and changed my attitude, so I thought I would share some of them with you.

- Proverbs 10:17b "But he who ignores reproof goes astray."
- Proverbs 12:1b "But he who hates reproof is stupid."
- Proverbs 13:18b "But he who regards reproof will be honored."
- Proverbs 15:5b "But he who regards reproof is sensible."
- Proverbs 15:10b "He who hates reproof will die."
- Proverbs 15:31 "He whose ear listens to the life-giving reproof will dwell among the wise."

These verses still mean a lot to me.

In discussing humility, it would be inexcusable not to mention Moses. Numbers 12:3 states "Now the man Moses was very humble, more than any man who was on the face of the earth." This verse comes in the middle of the story about when Aaron and Miriam became jealous of Moses. Aaron was so jealous that he said, "Can God only speak through Moses?" Aaron and Miriam thought they were just as important, and God dealt with their jealously by making Miriam leprous. Moses didn't respond by saying you brought it on yourselves or you just got what you deserved, but Moses cried to the Lord saying, "O God, heal her I pray."

Pride – the lost vice

If humility is the lost virtue, is pride the lost vice? The Bible talks about pride as the most deadly of sins. Solomon in Proverbs 11:2 states, "When pride comes, then comes dishonor, but with the humble is wisdom." St. Augustine of Hippo wrote, "Pride is the commencement of all sin because it was this which overthrew the devil, from whom arose the origin of sin."

Just as there was change in Christian thought about humility so also there has been change in the attitude about pride. I think this is especially concerning for us who have accomplished some things in our job or ministry over the years. We look back on those accomplishments with an air of pride. Neil Burton (2012) in a *Psychology Today* article titled, "Is Pride a Virtue or a Vice?" states "In short, be proud of your pride. Cultivate it. Give it free rein. Let it work for you." He clearly believes that pride is a virtue, and I think so do most of us today.

Gotquestions.org (2017) states, "There is a difference between the kind of pride that God hates (Proverbs 8:13) and the kind of pride we feel about a job well done. The kind of pride that stems from self-righteousness which is sin. Psalms 10:4 explains that the proud are so consumed with themselves that their thoughts are far from God." Gotquestions.org (2017) defines pride as "giving ourselves credit for something that God has accomplished… Pride is essentially self-worship. Anything we accomplished in this world would not have been possible were it not for God enabling and sustaining us." 1 Corinthians 4:7 states, "For who regards you as superior? What do you have that you did not receive? And if you did receive it, why do you boast as if you had not received it?" That's why God alone deserves the glory and not us. We are truly all on the same level before God. **All that we have and all that we are comes from Him!**

For this reason, we need to look back on our lives and give God the glory for any good thing that we received, and as a result, we should humbly serve our fellow man out of love for what God has done for us.

Matthew 23:12 "Whoever exalts himself shall be humbled; and whoever humbles himself shall be exalted."

Think about a time in your life when your pride caused you to fall.

I grew up in western Pennsylvania where pitching horseshoes was a favorite pastime. Many homes had horseshoe pits in their back yard and there were local teams that traveled for matches. I built a horseshoe court in our backyard and would practice a lot just for fun. I was recruited by our local team, and at the age of nineteen I was pitching horseshoes with the best in the world. I will never forget my last match. The games were won by the first team to reach 50 points. Many times, there would be four ringers on a peg, and then no one would score, as a ringer is worth 3 points if not eliminated by an opponent's ringer. My partner and I started strong. I threw 11 ringers out of my first 12 shoes and my partner was 6 for 12. We were winning 30 to 0, on our way to an easy victory. My opponent kept telling me how good I was, and I started to believe it. Anyway, I lost my touch, and they came back to win 50 to 48. That was a lifelong lesson I will never forget. Pride does come before a fall, and we fell hard.

***True Humility is not thinking less of yourself, it's thinking of yourself less.** – C.S. Lewis*

James 3:13 (NIV) "Who is wise and understanding among you? Let them show it by their good life, by deeds done in the humility that comes from wisdom.

Just in case there might be some misunderstanding about humility and pride I want to close this section with a quote from that great philosopher Yogi Berra, **"It ain't the heat, it's the humility."** ☺

Self-Control

Jerry Bridges (2006) states, "Self-control is the believer's wall of defense against sinful desires that wage war against the soul." Bridges (2006) explains that self-control is probably best defined as the governing of one's desires. He says, "Self-control is necessary because we are at war with our own sinful desires. What makes these sinful desires so dangerous is that they dwell within our own heart." Matthew 16:24 states, "Then Jesus said to His disciples, 'If anyone wishes to come after Me, he must deny himself, and take up his cross and follow Me.'" To be a follower of Christ, we need to deny ourselves. Andy Stanley says that denying ourselves means we deny or reject our own personal desires for our own good, like not taking that piece of cake. We need to be in control and not out of control. Proverbs 25:28 tells us that if we are not in control we are "Like a city that is broken into and without walls is a man who has no control over his spirit." If we lack self-control, our defenses will be broken down and the enemy will have easy access to us. He will be able to influence our behavior for his benefit. Perhaps, that is why Paul in Titus 2 specifically points out that self-control is something that both older men and older women should be concerned about.

Self-Control is not eating all your popcorn before the movie starts. ☺

Speech

How are we doing with self-control? Do we control our speech and our temper, or do we have a problem in this area? As I was researching this topic, I came across some questions posted on social media such as, "Why do old people feel they can say whatever they want?" Certainly, younger people think we are not very restrained when it comes to our speech, and we need to be more careful here. We might have less concern about what others think about us and that could be good, but we must still prioritize our concern about what God thinks of us. We are probably as much or maybe more prone to gossip than the younger. Ephesians 4:29a states, "Let no unwholesome word proceed from your mouth, but only such *a word* as is good." As we slowdown in our older age, we need also to slow down when we speak. ☺ Slow down, think about it, before we let that thought proceed out of our mouths.

Self-Control is knowing you can, but deciding you won't.

"Never miss a chance to shut-up." Chuck Swindol

"Leadership is a matter of having people look at you and gain confidence, seeing how you react. If you're in control, they're in control." Tom Landry

1 Corinthians 9:27, "but I discipline my body and make it my slave, so that, after I have preached to others, I myself will not be disqualified."

Anger

A few years ago, I was trying to help a church that was going through some difficult times. They asked me to look at their situation and give them counsel as to how they should move forward. Their staff and leader board was reduced in size, and one of the congregants seemed to have the most influence on the direction the church was headed. When discussing church issues, he would on occasion lose his temper and say it was just because he was passionate about what was happening. Looking back, I realized that I didn't recognize how destructive that was. Proverbs 29:11 states, "A fool always loses his temper, but a wise man holds it back." A wise person is not an angry person. Proverbs 17:27 states, "He who restrains his words has knowledge, and he who has a cool spirit is a man of understanding." We should then be a person with few words and a calm spirit to be able to influence others correctly.

A good friend of mine loves to play golf, but at times the game gets under his skin, and he throws his clubs. Golf can be a great revealer of our character, and throwing your clubs is not good for you or your fellow golfers. I talked to him, and he took it to heart that his Christian testimony was being brought down because of his lack of self-control. I would like to say he has stopped it completely, but he has improved a lot and talks about it with others as a problem that he has. Self-control can be challenging, but it's important if we are going to be the spiritual leaders we need to be.

By constant self-discipline and self-control you can develop greatness of character. - Grenville Kleiser

Proverbs 16:32 "He who is slow to anger is better than the mighty, and he who rules his spirit, than he who captures a city.

"Are We Fruitful?" Let's review:

Love – is a deliberate attitude. It is the foundation of all the other virtues. We can't love others without forgiving, and we as a group need to be recognized for our loving attitude.

Joy – is good medicine and helps our physical condition. We shouldn't let other Christians, our battle with the flesh, our loss of loved ones, or our struggle with physical issues to rob us of our joy. We need to consider it **all** joy.

Peace – We need to be at peace with God, within ourselves, and with other people. This should be our overriding attitude. We should have the presence of tranquility even in the midst of chaos. We should have peace about the future. We can't enjoy today if we are anxious about tomorrow.

Patience – We should be patient when responding to provocation, tolerating shortcomings in others, waiting on God, and persevering through adversity. We need to have a peaceful attitude while we are patiently waiting.

Kindness – It is best shown through generosity to others. We are the most generous age group. We need to continue to grow here as we encourage others to be generous. The major detriments to generosity are the desire to be rich, belief that money is the source of happiness, and believing that money brings security. If we generously give to God, and give out of love, we will be truly paying it forward and will receive eternal rewards.

Goodness – The act of being truly good is found in our inner character which should reflect the character of God. We as individuals or as a nation cannot be good without God. Integrity seems to be dissolving with the younger generations, and we need to lead in this area. We can show integrity through doing life. We can teach it though stories, and we can transfer it through leadership opportunities.

Faithfulness – We need to be faithful up and until we take our last breath. We need to be obedient, develop our God given gifts, keep our promises, and pass on what we have learned.

Gentleness – It is best shown through humility. Humility is the lost virtue. It was once the key virtue of the Christian faith but it has now been pushed aside and it is considered a weakness and not a strength. If humility is the lost virtue, then pride is the lost vice. Pride is no longer the sin that besets us just as it did the devil and caused him to be thrown out of heaven. We think we are self-made and not God-made.

Self-Control – It is our wall of defense against sinful desires. We first need to control our speech. We need to deal with our thought life and understand that everything we think does not need to flow out of our mouth. We need to close that door and say only the things that build others up. We also need to control our anger and have a cool spirit.

- Are We Valuable?
- Are We Fruitful?
- Are We Using Our Time Wisely?
- Are We Helping the Younger?

In the first section, we learned we indeed are valuable and society and hopefully the church is starting to realize that. More importantly we are valuable to God even though we may not feel like we are. Remember from chapter 3, Psalms 92: 12-15 "the righteous man (or woman) will flourish like the palm tree; he will grow like a cedar in Lebanon. Planted in the house of the Lord, they will flourish in the courts of our God. **They will still yield fruit in old age**; they shall be full of sap and very green. To declare that the Lord is upright; He is my rock, and there is no unrighteousness in Him."

Galatians 5:22-26 "But the fruit of the Spirit is love, joy, peace, patience, kindness, goodness, faithfulness, gentleness, self-control. Against such things there is not law. Those who belong to Christ Jesus have crucified the sinful nature with its passions and desires. Since we live by the Spirit, let us keep in step with the Spirit. Let us not become conceited, provoking and envying each other."

Our value is most dependent on our spiritual maturity, hence the section on "Are We Fruitful?" Are we bearing fruit internally? Are we being changed by the Holy Spirit and becoming more like Christ? If we are being changed and growing spiritually, that growth will impact what we do and how we affect the lives of others. After we have looked at who we are, next we will look at what we do.

Certainly, who we are is more important than what we do, but we can't ignore our actions. Everything we do is in response to what we believe and should show gratitude for what Christ has done for us, especially at this time in our lives. Most of us have finished a career (maybe 2 or 3), married, and raised children. Now, we think we are done. **Ah, not so Kemosobe!** ☺ (For those of us who remember the Lone Ranger and Tonto)

Instead of viewing this time of our lives as being done, time to rest, or no longer useful, we need to view it as the greatest opportunistic time of our lives. We have a new-found freedom and are not burdened with a job or raising children. This can truly be the most rewarding and exciting time of our lives. We can bear fruit in our old age and serve our God in ways we never thought or expected.

Abraham and Sara thought they were too old to be the father and mother of a multitude of people, but they were wrong, and so are we when we think we are too old! Now is the time to step out for Christ. We truly can do **all** things through Christ who strengthens us (Philippians 4:13). I believe if we stand together, we can turn our nation and the American church around. But first, let's look at what we should be doing. In this next section, we will look at how we typically spend our time and how we need to change. We need to view our time as one of our greatest resources. Then we will look at the value of serving others, praying, teaching/studying, and sharing the gospel. We can do new things, and this could be the most exciting time of our lives. Again, let's transition into heaven going full steam and not just limping along. Let's evaluate, **"Are we spending our time wisely?"**

ARE WE USING OUR TIME WISELY?

Chapter 9

As Time is a Great Resource

Colossians 4:5(ESV) "Walk in wisdom toward outsiders, making the best use of the time."

Have you ever said, "I just lost track of the time?" Or, maybe you said "I just lost myself in a book and the time just flew by." **Life can be just like that!** Before you know it, it's over. Your time is running out, the clock is ticking. If you still have a watch, look at the second hand, you can actually see your time slipping away. Every time that second hand moves, it's another second that you will never get back. How gruesome is that! Andy Stanley tells the story of your life. First you are born, and then you attend grade school, and then high school. You probably go to college, get a job, get married, and have kids. Then put your kids through college, retire from your job, play golf, and die. Stanley also said your time is running out, and the older we get, the faster it seems to fly by. I can remember my grandfather talking about how time goes by faster when you get older. Instead of talking about yesterday, we are talking about something 10, 20, 40, or 50 years ago, just like it was yesterday, because to us it does seem like yesterday. In some ways, it seems just like yesterday that Carol and I were married, and this past June we celebrated our 53rd wedding anniversary. At Christmas time, my grandfather would say "didn't we just celebrate Christmas last week?" At least it seemed like last week.

Time does go faster the older we get because our life is the measuring stick of time. At one year old, the next year will be 50% of our life. At 10 years, the next year is 10% and at 50 years the next year is only 2%. So, it really does go faster. ☺

We are also very obsessed with time. We are constantly saying "what time is it?" We are always focused on it. We hate to wait in line, or wait for our food at a restaurant, and we are so frustrated with our computer because it is **so slow**. We go out and upgrade our computer to the latest technology in order to speed it up, because it is wasting our time and driving us crazy.

How we spend our time is important! That was the primary principle behind God establishing the Sabbath for the Jews. It wasn't just that He was interested in their time one day a week but that all their time was important, and one day was especially committed to Him. Ephesians 5:16 states that we should make the most of our time. It is important, especially since our time on earth is short. Job said, "How my days are swifter than a runner; they flee away." (Job 9:25a) James 4:14b states, "You are a just a vapor that appears for a little while and then vanishes away." It's just like a little puff of smoke that is here for an instance then disappears. Our life is short compared to eternity. Whether we live to 20, 40, 60, or 80, it is still short, but I do think 100 is old. ☺

Andy Stanley says there is a point in your life where you no longer think about how old you are but about how much time you have left. We start sensing that there is a finish line. For me, it was in the spring of 2001, age 55. I had been experiencing pain down my arm and had been to the doctor a couple of times, but I wasn't ready for surgery. Carol and my doctor were ready, but I thought I could get through another season of softball before I had to go under the knife and have neck fusion. At our first practice that spring I was up to bat during a practice scrimmage. I took a hard swing, and as the bat hit the ball I felt a sharp pain down my arm that really got my attention. I then told the guys I had to take a season off and arranged the surgery. I know neck fusion is not as traumatic as some other kinds of surgeries, but for me it was an eye opener. I realized that my body was starting to go through the aging process, and at some time I would have to give it up. That was the turning point for me. How many years would I have left? But even more important than that, how am I going to spend the time I have left. Stanley says there is a web site, deathclock.com, where you can find out how much time you have left. How gruesome is that? ☹

Even though our time is running out and our time on earth is short, for us, **time could be our greatest resource!** Just think about it. We are no longer raising kids, we are probably retired from our job, and our church and community responsibilities are probably less. **We have time!** And it could be **a lot** of time. A study from the Society of Actuaries (Pfan, 2106) states that from a healthy 65-year-old couple, one will probably live to be 92, and there is a 25% chance they could live to be 97. If we are 65 there is a good chance that we could live to be 95. **We could have 30 more years!!** Now, relatively speaking, that's **a lot** of time.

At the time of this writing, the oldest living person in the US is 115 years old. Some others outside the US without documented birth certificates claim to be 126 or 127 years old. Whatever remaining time God gives us, we all want to use it wisely.

Jesus gives us a great parable in Matthew 25 that demonstrates wisdom in time usage. It's the parable of the talents, and it implies that God gives us all a measure of talents to put to good use. Jesus tells us about three slaves and how they handled the talents given them from the master. The first two slaves received 5 and 2 talents respectively, and after they received them they went out and earned more talents. They used their time and resources to gain more talents for the master. The third slave received one talent but did not use his time wisely and just hid the talent that was given him. He wasted the talent and his time. When the master returned, he praised the first two slaves, "Well done, good and faithful slave. You were faithful with a few things, I will put you in charge of many things; enter into the joy of your master." (Matthew 25:21) But for the third slave the master called him "a wicked and lazy slave" (Matthew 25:26). None of us wants to be viewed as lazy; we all want to be productive for the master. But first, let's look at how we typically spend our time.

I looked at an article taken from the *Monthly Labor Review*, dated May, 2007. The title of the article was "How do older Americans spend their time?" (Krantz-Kent & Stewart). I know that we Christians are not typical Americans, but the culture and society does influence us. The numbers might be different for us, but I would expect the trends to be the same. Krantz-Kent and Stewart (2007) look at aging men and women going from 55 to over 70 years old and how they spend their time as they age. They also look at the effect of working full time, working part time, and not working. You probably fall somewhere within their study. For men as they age from 55 to over 70 and are retired, they spend less time doing housework, like gardening, cleaning, and painting. They spend more time watching TV. Actually, it almost goes up 50%. They spend more time relaxing, up 50% and less time exercising, down 20%. They spend less time socializing, down 30% and everything else (religious activity, travel, sleep, grooming/eating) is pretty much the same. For men working part time during this time, the difference from not working is that they exercise less, watch TV less, do less housework, and volunteer less. If they are still working full time, during this time the trends are the same as working part time only greater. They spend more time working and less time doing the other activities, which makes sense. For women, the trends are the same as for men except they spend more time doing housework, less time watching TV, and less time exercising than men.

The one statistic that stands out for both men and women is that when we age we do not increase our religious activities and it doesn't matter if we work full time, part time, or not at all. We exchange our work time with watching TV, doing house work, and relaxing (Krantz-Kent & Stewart, 2007). How sad is that! I wonder if that puts us in the same category as the wicked slave.

In light of this information, how do we change? How do we make the most of this tremendous resource, **TIME**?

Certainly, changing the way we live and spend our time is not easy. Let me rephrase that. **It's not easy to change to doing it the right way.** We can always fill up our time doing all kinds of things. Like the recently retired person who says, "How did I ever have time to work?" Let's look at three steps to help us in changing the way we use our time.

Planning your time

The first step is to plan your time. We must take time to plan our time. If we don't think about it, we will waste our time. Put time aside to plan. In my working years with IBM, I was surprised to see that the president of IBM had 1 – 1 ½ hours in his time each day for thinking and planning. That's how it was listed on his daily planner. (We're the only ones who know what a daily planner is. ☺) His time was so valuable that he set aside some time to plan it! Your time is the same. It is extremely valuable, and we need to plan it, both short term and long term. If this is something that you never have done before, stop reading right now and take some time to plan your time. Before you do, pray and ask for God's help.

After today, plan on a daily time to plan your time. I do it either during my morning devotions or right after. I think about my day, and plan and evaluate my long-term usage of time. I probably don't do this every day, and I don't necessarily get it right, but I try.

Evaluating your time

Second, when you are planning your time, first evaluate how you are presently doing. Moses said in Psalms 90:12a, "So teach us to number our days." John MacArthur (2006) says this means to "evaluate the use of time in light of the brevity of life." As we evaluate our use of time, be sensitive to God's leading. Proverbs 16:9 states, "Man plans his way but God directs his steps." It's ok to plan your time, but be sensitive to God in the direction that He is leading, and always pray for wisdom in the process.

As we evaluate, remember we are highly influenced by the culture and the tyranny of the urgent. If something interferes with our plans, be sure it is God's redirection. Don't just fall into the demands and suggestions of others, but do use others' opinions in the evaluation process. Perhaps, **we just need to stop doing some things.**

In one of my IBM management schools, they told us to put our mail into three piles in order of priority, A, B, and C. Then, they said divide the B pile into either the A or C as everything can either be high or low priority so that you only have two piles left. Then, they said to **throw away the C pile!** We should do the same with our time. Just stop doing some things, or at least cut back. Some things just waste our time. But always be in the evaluating process and do get input from those closest to you. A wise man looks for and receives wise counsel.

Ephesians 5:15-16 states, "Therefore be careful how you walk, not as unwise men but as wise, **making the most of your time**, because the days are evil. We need to make the most of our time well aware that the days are evil. We can certainly relate to the evil days. We can see the moral decline of the US, and how we as a nation are turning away from God. How the churches are watering down God's Word, and how integrity seems to be a lost art. But in light of the fact that the days are evil, **we have a great opportunity**. The Amplified Bible of the same passage reads, "Buying up each opportunity." John MacArthur (2006) states, "The Greek word for time denotes a fixed, measured, allocated season. We are to make the most of our time on this evil earth in fulfilling God's purposes, lining up every opportunity for useful worship and service." Don't focus on the evil days but on the **opportunities**. Maybe we need to cut back on Fox news and look for the opportunities that are available to us.

Prioritize our time

Third and finally we should prioritize our time. Andy Stanley states that **priority determines capacity.** If you prioritize correctly, you can get more accomplished. His visual example is to take a small box and fill it with rocks. The small rocks represent the "busy" things in our life that seemingly waste our time. The medium rocks represent the good things that can be beneficial to do in the right quantity, like playing golf ☺ or shopping, mine and Carol's most favorite things to do. The larger rocks represent the most important things in our life, like serving God, studying the Bible, helping family, and serving others.

If you put the small rocks in first, the way most of us prioritize, and the medium rocks second, the big rocks won't fit. If you put the big rocks in first, then the medium, you have lots of room for the small rocks. Priority determines capacity. If we respond to all the urgent things first, we have no time for the important things.

Martin Luther "I have so much to do that I shall spend the first three hours in prayer."

I have said before that our time is running out and that is true, but have you ever stopped to think that you might be able to get more time? Your first thought is, *that is crazy.* We can't get more time. When our time is up, it's up. God determines when that time is and there is nothing we can do about it. Certainly, God determines the length of our days, but maybe we have some flexibility here. We exercise, have surgery, get chemo treatments, eat vegetables, and the like to get more time. We want to live a healthy life because we know that those who live a healthy life generally live longer. In addition to living healthily, I'm going to give you three more ways to get more time.

Socializing

The first is being in community: socializing. It is important to be socially engaged throughout the aging process. Staying connected to others and maintaining socially supportive relationships have both been shown to enhance the mental and physical health of the elderly and to contribute to longevity. The time study showed that both men and women actually socialize less as they get older instead of more (Krantz-Kent & Stewart 2007). We tend to stay home more and travel or get out less. So being in a neighborhood that does a lot together is good. We live in a 55+ golf community, and there are always a variety of activities. We have a multitude of clubs and a great clubhouse to swim, exercise, take classes, eat, and play games. A lot of activity is centered around golf, and we really care for each other, the way neighborhoods used to.

Be active in a Christian community, not only just attending a good church but in a small group and if possible in a senior adult community. Our senior adult community is a caring family. We pray for each other, help each other, and serve God together. So being in community is important.

Obedience

Second is to be obedient to God. Obedience brings longevity. Proverbs 3:1b-2: "But let your heart keep my commandments; for length of days and years of life and peace they will add to you." As we are obedient, we grow in our love and reverence for God. Proverbs 10:27a: "The fear of the Lord prolongs life." Obedience and reverence along with wisdom can give us more time. Proverbs 3:16: "Long life is in her (Wisdom's) right hand."

Praying

The third and final way to extend your life is with prayer. As we pray for wisdom, we could also pray for a long life. Hezekiah was told that he was going to die, so he prayed for more time, and God gave him 15 more years.

- Hezekiah's prayer - Isaiah 38: 1-3 "In those days Hezekiah became mortally ill, and Isaiah the prophet came to him and said to him, thus says the Lord, 'Set your house in order, for you shall die and not live.' Then Hezekiah turned his face to the wall and prayed to the Lord."

- God's response - Isaiah 38:5b "I have heard your prayer, I have seen your tears; behold I will add 15 years to your life"

I pray daily that God will give us (Carol and me) long lives to impact others for Christ. God did it for Hezekiah, and He could do it for you and me. Again, God determines the length of our days, and He can even increase them. ☺

ARE WE USING OUR TIME WISELY?

Chapter 10

By Praying

Proverbs 15:8b "**But the prayer of the upright is His (God's) delight.**"

Ok, you're thinking a chapter on prayer – great. You have read books on prayer, learned outlines on how to pray, listened to sermons on prayer, been in prayer groups, and now more on prayer. Why?

If we consider how we can best use our time in this stage of our life, what can be more important than praying? Prayer is the most important thing we can do, and it probably could be the last thing we will be able to do. If our mind remains, but our body declines, prayer could be the only thing we can do to impact the kingdom. We have studied it, been preached to about it, talked about it, but when asked what's the greatest problem in the church today 1,300 evangelical leaders said **PRAYER** (Deaton, 2006)**.** If lack of prayer is the greatest problem, then prayer must also be the greatest solution.

The greatest problem in the church is a lack of prayer, and I think it is also true in our country. We, as a society, decided we no longer wanted God in it, so we are now paying the price. After the decision to remove prayer from our schools in 1962, our moral downfall as a society has been significant. According to inplainsite.org:

- Pregnancies in girls ages 10-14 have increased by 553%
- The divorce rate in marriages has increased 300%
- Single parent families with children are up 160%
- Violent crime has increased 544% (Brooks, 2107).

So, the greatest need in our churches and our society is prayer. Even with this great reason to pray, there are others just as significant.

God wants us to pray

Paul encourages us to pray. 1Timothy 2:1: "First of all, then, I urge that entreaties *and* prayers, petitions *and* thanksgivings, be made on behalf of all men." Paul says that God wants us to pray for everyone, and He wants us to pray because that act of communication pleases Him. God views our prayers as a sweet-smelling aroma.

In an article published in 1888 by J.R. Miller on "The Sweet Fragrance of Prayer," Miller tells us that "true prayer is fragrant to God." He states the example of the golden-incense altar in the Old Testament Tabernacle/Temple was the altar of prayer, and now every believer's loving heart is a golden altar from which rise up to God a sweet fragrance. In Revelation 5:8, the redeemed are represented as "holding golden bowls full of incense which are the prayers of the saints." Miller states that this represents the earth's supplications which rise up into heaven as sweet incense. This shows that the prayers of believers are very precious in the sight of God and He values them highly. The fact that God views our prayers in this way should be a great motivator to us. We seem to disappoint God constantly and fall short so often in other areas, but here we can truly please Him and be pleasing to Him even when we do fall short.

Jesus as our example prayed

Jesus taught us to pray as well as giving us a great example. He often would pray for several hours at a time and challenged His disciples to pray.

- Luke 5:16 "But Jesus Himself would *often* slip away to the wilderness and pray."
- Luke 6:12 "It was at this time that He went off to the mountain to pray, and He spent the whole night in prayer to God."

This example should be an incentive for us to pray more. Certainly, we should not pray in vain repetitions but we should pray more. When my third grandchild was being born at 30 weeks, I tried to pray all night for his life. I didn't make it all night, but I gave it a good effort. Zac is now in college and doing great.

Evaluate how much you actually do pray in a week and increase it; maybe double it, because of Christ's example and the fact that it is pleasing to God.

It brings us closer to God

I am not much of a talker. To carry on a conversation just for the sake of talking doesn't seem to motivate me. The conversation should be about something important: to solve some major problem or to rehash a sporting event. This has been quite a challenge for my wonderful wife, Carol, of 53 years. Without communication, a marriage will be severely strained. To rectify that, she has learned the skill of asking me questions, not necessarily because she needs the information, but because she wants to keep our relationship on track. She had to overcome my lack of communication skills, and she has done a great job. She understood the importance of communication more than I did. I am still weak in this area but after 53 years there has been some improvement. ☺ James 4:8: "Draw near to God and He will draw near to you." If we want to be closer to God, we must be the initiator through prayer. If we pray to draw closer to God, He will draw close to us. Just talk to Him. Tell Him how wonderful He is and just pray, not because you have an urgent need or desire information but just because you want to be closer to Him.

As a side note, I was never like the guy who said he didn't have to keep telling his wife he loved her, because he told her when they got married, and if it changed he would let her know. At least I don't think so, maybe you should ask Carol. ☺

God hears our prayers

Did you ever try to talk to someone, and he or she was preoccupied with something or someone else? Maybe the person was listening to another conversation or just thinking about something else. How frustrating is that? Probably part of my lack of communication skill is that I am always thinking about something. I am usually solving a problem of some kind or another, and I need to be shocked out of my thoughts to communicate. We never have to do that with God. Psalms 77:1: "My voice rises to God, and I will cry aloud; my voice rises to God, and He will hear me." **God is never too busy for us.** He can listen to all of us at the same time. I wish I could just do two things at once. When Carol talks to me, I must stop the TV to focus on her conversation. This is not necessary with God. He doesn't have to stop one communication in order to listen to someone else. He is always there, waiting for us, and His cell tower never drops a call.

God responds to our prayers

We live at a time when we as Christians don't seem to get a response from those in governmental leadership. Our desires are ignored, and our ability to talk openly about our faith and issues that violate Godly principles continues to be limited. We feel like the government doesn't care and doesn't agree with our concerns. This is not so with God. Psalms 81:7a: "You (Israel) called in trouble and I (God) rescued you." God responded to the prayers of Israel, and He will respond to our prayers. He may not do what we ask, or He may take a lot longer than we want, but He listens and responds like a loving father to his child.

Matthew 7:7-11: "Ask, and it will be given to you; seek, and you will find; knock, and it will be opened to you. For everyone who asks receives, and he who seeks finds, and to him who knocks it will be opened. Or what man is there among you who, when his son asks for a loaf, will give him a stone? Or if he asks for a fish, he will not give him a snake, will he? If you then, being evil, know how to give good gifts to your children, how much more will your Father who is in heaven give what is good to those who ask Him!"

God is the perfect father; He will certainly respond to us. Sometimes we as children ask for things that would not be good for us, so God says no. I liken that situation to the five-year-old who asks for the keys to the car. God knows what's best for us, and we need to trust Him.

My mother at the age of 46 was diagnosed with ovarian cancer. The doctor tried to operate, but the tumor was too large to remove, and it eventually took her life. We prayed hard for God to heal her, but she continued to get worse. It was at her bed side that I prayed publicly for the first time. She would ask me to pray, and I did, no matter who was in the room. I prayed for God to keep her alive, and He did for quite some time. We had no idea how long she could survive this way, so we continued to pray until one day God just impressed on me that she would not survive this disease. That same day, I asked God not to let her suffer any longer. I knew she was a believer and would be in heaven when she died. As near as I can tell, at the same time I prayed, she took a turn for the worse and died within 24 hours. As a child, I didn't understand God's best, I just needed to trust Him.

It's a cure for anxiety

In chapter 5, I discussed how anxiety can rob us of our joy and peace. Anxiety can be a crippling disease that can ruin our lives. It's also contagious. We seem to be affected by the anxiety of others, and in the same way, our anxiety will stimulate anxiety in others. But again, God gives us the answer. Philippians 4:6: "Be anxious for nothing, but in everything by prayer and supplication with thanksgiving let your requests be made known to God." The cure for anxiety is prayer. The greater your anxiety, the more you need to pray, and again, pray with thanksgiving. Be more thankful in your prayers, and the anxiety disease will go away or at least be reduced.

Several years ago, I was traveling on business to Vietnam. Vietnam was a long way from my small home town of Sterling, Virginia, and the experience of being in a communist country was new to me. I had two trips there, and at the close of my second trip, I wanted to get home as soon as possible. My colleagues wanted to stay another day, so I decided to travel home alone. I left the evening after our last business meeting, and my trip home went from Hanoi to Saigon to Bangkok to Tokyo to Chicago and then to Washington D.C. I started on my journey, and in traveling from Hanoi to Saigon, I learned that the airline I was flying to Bangkok just went on strike, and the stewardesses on my present flight were not interested in my problems. As I arrived in the domestic terminal at Saigon, I was anxiously waiting for my luggage and praying a lot about my situation. I didn't know the language or my way around. I was in the domestic terminal, and my next flight didn't exist. As I stood there beside an Asian man, I nervously started up a conversation not knowing if he could even speak English. I asked him where he was from, I assumed he lived in the area, but his answer was most amazing when he said, "Sterling, Virginia." He didn't say the USA or Virginia or Washington D.C., but Sterling, Virginia. I felt a flood of emotion come over me that seemed to be a message from God that said, "I can take care of you no matter where you are." The man lived about 1-2 miles from my house, and he was a regional manager for Fed Ex.in Vietnam. He would work over there for 6 weeks and then come back home to Virginia for a couple of weeks. I told him my plight, and he got on his phone and took care of me. He got me to the right place where I had to stay overnight and got a flight out the next day. Not only was my anxiety cured but also my travel problems – God is good!

Our prayers accomplish much

Our prayers are far more valuable than we think. To think they can move the heart of God, how great is that! James 5:16b: "The effective prayer of a righteous man can accomplish much." Our prayers can accomplish much.

I will never forget how God answered our prayers regarding our son, Ryan. When Ryan was 9 years old, he became sick, and we thought it was just something that was going around. It happened to be just before Christmas, and he was lying on the couch while we were watching on TV the lighting of the National Christmas tree. Ryan then proceeded to say they were throwing things at him from the TV. We didn't know what to do, so we waited until morning, and took him to our family doctor. Much to our surprise, the doctor said that Ryan's appendix had ruptured, and we needed to rush him to the hospital right away. Ryan went through surgery fine, and I didn't think to bother God as it all seemed to be working out. We took him home. The next day, his fever spiked up, and he started to cough. So, we rushed him back to the hospital. I'll never forget walking down the hall with the surgeon and seeing the fear in his eyes as he explained to me that sometimes the poison gets into other vital organs, and they can't stop it. So, before the second surgery, I was brought to my knees, and I prayed hard for the life of my son. He again went through surgery fine, his fever dropped right away, and I learned a valuable life lesson.

God gives us forgiveness

God is eager to grant us forgiveness; all we must do is ask for it. 1 John 1:9: "If we confess our sins, He is faithful and righteous to forgive us our sins and to cleanse us from all unrighteousness." This doesn't mean that our salvation is dependent on our daily seeking God's forgiveness for our every sin. Once we put our faith in Christ as our Lord and Savior, we are eternally forgiven for all past and future sins. But what it does mean is that a true believer will be always confessing his sin before God. John MacArthur

(2006) states, "Continual confession of sin is an indication of genuine salvation." This daily confession will also determine how God deals with us daily. Matthew 6:14, 15: "For if you forgive others for their transgressions, your heavenly Father will also forgive you. But if you do not forgive others, then your Father will not forgive your transgressions." This applies to our daily life and not our eternal position. God will deal with us daily in the same way we deal with others. We need to seek forgiveness through prayer and grant forgiveness to others.

To be effective in our prayer life we need to pray secretly and sincerely

Pray Secretly

The disciples asked, and Jesus taught them how to pray. Matthew 6:6: "But you, when you pray, go into your inner room, close your door and pray to your Father who is in secret, and your Father who sees what is done in secret will reward you."

We must first pray secretly. That doesn't mean we shouldn't pray publicly but in secret is where we are most effective. Go into your room, close the door, find a closet, office, workshop, or out in the garage. Seek some secret place away from people and alone with God. Get away from distractions as best you can. Distractions will take our thoughts away from God. Don't try to fight distractions, as best you can try to avoid them. I use my office and close the door. The place where you pray will over time create a special atmosphere for you because it is where you best communicate with God. Go there during your best time of the day, morning, evening, or whenever you feel most alert.

Several years ago, when I was working at IBM, I used to have my devotions at lunch time in my office. That worked ok most of the time, but some days I couldn't take a lunch break, or I was traveling so I would miss. Also, I did not usually work on the week-ends, so I would miss again. It took me awhile to realize that the only things I do the same each day are go to bed and get up in the mornings. I started to get up a little earlier each day, and I have been able to keep that habit over several years. I also get up on the week-ends, so I could close that door as well. ☺

Pray Sincerely

Mean what we say. Matthew 6:7, 8: "And when you are praying, do not use meaningless repetition as the Gentiles do, for they suppose they will be heard for their many words. Do not be like them, for your Father knows what you need before you ask Him." Do not use meaningless repetition. Just talk, and be careful of clichés that don't mean anything like "please be with me." Hebrews 13:5b states, "I will never desert you, nor will I ever leave you." God will always be with you. As we understand Scripture better, we will be able to communicate more effectively with God. Simply talk to God as to a friend or father, authentically, reverently, personally, earnestly. Psalms 62:8: "Pour out your heart to God." Talk to the Father sincerely.

When talking about the apostle Paul, E.M. Bounds (2001) stated "His teaching is that praying is the most important of all things on earth. All else must be restrained, retired, to give it primacy. Put it first, keep its primacy. If prayer is put first, then God is put first, and victory is assured."

A friend of mine, Scott Darling, started a prayer ministry for the persecuted church. If you would like to receive his updates, please contact Scott at One@OneMillionPraying.org.

Talking to men for God is a great thing, but talking to God for men is greater still." E.M. Bounds

You can do more than pray after you have prayed; but you can never do more than pray until you have prayed." A.J. Gordon

Don't pray when you feel like it. Have an appointment with the Lord and keep it. A man is powerful on his knees." Corrie ten Boom

The little estimate we put on prayer is evidence from the little time we give to it." E.M. Bounds

- Proverbs 15:29 "The LORD is far from the wicked, but He hears the prayer of the righteous."
- Psalms 145:18 "The LORD is near to all who call upon Him, to all who call upon Him in truth."

Challenge:

Prayer is the most important and possibly the last thing we will be able to do on this earth. This chapter was most difficult for me as I increasingly realize how much I fall short in the area of prayer. **So, please join me and commit to spend more time on our knees, perhaps doubling what you do now.**

ARE WE USING OUR TIME WISELY?

Chapter 11

By Studying and Teaching the Bible

Hebrews 4:12 "For the Word of God is living and active and sharper than any two-edged sword, and piercing as far as the division of soul and spirit, of both joints and marrow, and able to judge the thoughts and intentions of the heart."

If prayer is the most important use of our time; studying, learning, and teaching the Word of God must be a close second. Actually, learning in general is very important at this time in our life. In a Gallup poll, they stated that one of the secrets to success in older adults is getting more education. The organization "Lifelong Learning" is committed to the task of continuing education for older adults. In an article by Nancy Merz Nordstrom she states that "Scientific research from the 1990's now reveals that more than ever before, a challenged, stimulated brain may be the key to a vibrant later life." Nancy lists some benefits to learning later in life. Some of which are:

- Lifelong learning increases our wisdom.
- Lifelong learning helps us find meaning in our lives.
- Lifelong learning leads to an enriching life of self-fulfillment.

If just learning in general can have this kind of an impact on our lives, just imagine what continued learning of the Word of God could do! So in this chapter, I want to look at some of the reasons why learning God's Word is especially important for us. Before I do let's look at some of the reasons why we don't study the Bible.

WHY DON'T WE STUDY THE BIBLE?

We don't think there is value in it

The number of Americans who are skeptical towards the Bible continues to rise. According to a 2014 Barna survey the number of those who are skeptical or agnostic toward the Bible (who believes that the Bible is "just another book of teachings written by men that contains stories and advice) has nearly doubled going from 10% to 19% in just three years. I believe this increase in skepticism of those outside the Christian faith affects us in a negative way. We think the Bible has lost its life changing value. Also, the percentage of Americans who believe the Bible is sacred has also fallen in the same three years, going from 86% in 2011 to 79% in 2014 according to the same survey.

We don't think we have enough time

In the Barna survey, the number one frustration among Bible readers is that they never have enough time just to read the Bible let alone study it. In just one year from 2013 to 2014, the percentage went from 40% to 47% who claimed a time problem. This could certainly have been a problem in our younger adult years when we were balancing family, job, and ministry responsibilities; but in our present life stage, time is an available resource as I stated in chapter 9. The problem is that we developed a habit of not studying the Bible and that just carried over. Now we have time!

We are afraid

Perhaps we are afraid that God will convict us of some activity and we will need to change, and that scares us. How crazy is that! Or maybe we are afraid of being in a group Bible study because we are embarrassed about our lack of Bible knowledge. Pride is certainly destructive, and we should find an environment where we can be comfortable so we can learn.

I led a Tuesday night Bible study for men in my community, mostly golfers, but not all. One of my fellow golfers, Nick Harris, started to attend and after several weeks he decided to drop out. I met with Nick, and he said he felt overwhelmed by his lack of Bible knowledge. He had decided to study the Bible on his own until he felt he could come back. I told him that it's difficult to just study on your own, and that he needed some accountability. I offered to go through the Operation Timothy project from CBMC (Christian Business Men's Connection) as it was structured for a one on one type of study. We did that and Nick loved it. We went through all 21 lessons, and he felt comfortable enough to come back to the Tuesday night study. He actually led some lessons. Nick became a close friend and brother in Christ. But shortly after he came back, to the group he suffered a stroke as a result of Chemotherapy, and he now is with the Lord. I miss him a lot and will look forward to seeing him again in heaven.

We think that ignorance is bliss

We think if we don't know what's wrong we won't get punished for doing the wrong thing. Have you ever said or thought "what I don't know won't hurt me." I didn't know there was ice on the road ahead and I still had an accident. Remember the story of David bringing back the ark of God. He did it the wrong way. In the process of transporting the ark, it almost upset and Uzzah reached out and took hold of it to keep it from falling (2 Samuel 6:6). He didn't know it was wrong but the anger of the Lord burned against him and God stuck him down for his irreverence. Uzzah's lack of knowledge that no one could touch the ark didn't save him. What he didn't know did hurt him and as a result he lost his life. We need to understand the Bible so we won't do the wrong thing out of ignorance.

We are lazy

OK, maybe this one is a little too personal, but if I think it's my problem then maybe you might as well. We can come up with a lot of excuses to support our lack of initiative, Proverbs 26:13 states, "The sluggard says, "There is a lion in the road! A lion is in the open square!" The lazy person makes up outlandish excuses that may or may not be true. He is also defensive. Proverbs 26:16 states, "The sluggard is wiser in his own eyes than seven men who can give a discreet answer." He thinks he is wiser by defending his behavior and not acknowledging it. So, being lazy is not an excuse. ☺

We think we have arrived

A lot of us have been attending church, Sunday school, and small groups for most of our life, and we think we know enough about the Bible. We seem to know more than our neighbors even though we don't talk about it much. So, how much more can we learn that would be beneficial? In a 2010 survey by the PEW Research Center when people were asked 12 questions about the Bible and Christianity, those who identified themselves as atheist or agnostic got an average of 6.7 questions right. What is shocking is that those who said they were Christian got an average of 6.2 questions right!

Remember 79% of Americans think the Bible is sacred and 56% think the Bible is the actual Word Of God but only 37% even read it once a week. **Folks we are in deep trouble!** No wonder the country doesn't know the difference between right and wrong. We think we are knowledgeable and we are not, just like the Corinthians where Paul challenged them in 1 Corinthians 8:2. He stated, "If anyone imagines that he knows something, he does not yet know as he ought to know." (ESV) We imagine we know a lot **but actually we know little!** Let's now look at some of the reasons why we should study the Bible.

WHY WE SHOULD STUDY THE BIBLE

Because it is God's Word

As I said before, Americans mostly view the Bible in a positive way and actually 56% view it as God's Word, but only 37% even read it once a week. Maybe we mentally agree that the Bible is God's Word but it doesn't get down to our heart. Then, **do we really believe it?** Actually the Bible teaches that we do what we believe.

If we really believe something to be true, we will act on it. Our beliefs precede our actions. We have been taught the Bible is God's Word. We've seen the internal and external evidences that show the Bible is God's Word. So we mentally believe it to be true but, **do we really believe it?**

God has miraculously preserved for us His message on how to live in this life and how to spend eternity in heaven. God knows us better than we know ourselves. He has told us all about Himself and us. His Word is truly sharper than any two-edged sword. It will reach into the depths of our being and change us to be more like Him.

- **God commands us to read it**

John tells us to "search the scriptures" (John 5:39). Recently in my men's community Bible study, one of the men said he gets more confused when he reads the Bible. He reads it every day and looks at various commentaries but is discouraged when they don't agree. Sometimes the more we study the more we realize how much we don't know. The benefits of Bible study far outweigh the draw backs even when the experts don't agree. God would not tell us to search the scriptures if continued study would not help us. So, continue to go deeper and God will give understanding.

- **God wrote it**

The Bible was written over a period of 1500 years by 35-40 different authors. God wrote it by inspiring or breathing it out through certain men. 2 Timothy 3:16, 17 states, "All Scripture is inspired by God and profitable for teaching, for reproof, for correction, for training in righteousness; [17] so that the man of God may be adequate, equipped for every good work." God wrote it and preserved it for our benefit. Sometimes, God told the Bible writers the exact words to say as He did with Jeremiah, "Then the LORD stretched out His hand and touched my mouth, and the LORD said to me, 'Behold, I have put My words in your mouth.'" (Jeremiah 1:9) But more often He used their minds, vocabularies, and experiences to produce His own perfect, infallible, inerrant Word. This inspiration applies only to the original autographs of Scripture, not the Bible writers or various translations.

- **God wants us to know Him better**

God has revealed Himself to us through creation as Paul states in Romans and that is beneficial but God has given us so much more through His Word. We need to grasp hold of it in the same way that Jacob wouldn't let God go when he wrestled with God all night. John 5:39b states, "it is these (the Scriptures) that testify about Me (Jesus)." The Scriptures are the best way to learn about God.

Because it changes us

- **Gives us wisdom**

Proverbs is especially targeted to give us wisdom, but so is the rest of the Bible. Proverbs 1:1-3 states, "The proverbs of Solomon the son of David, king of Israel: To know wisdom and instruction, to discern the sayings of understanding, to receive instruction in wise behavior, righteousness, justice and equity." Just as God gave Solomon wisdom, He will also give it to us through the study of His Word. Psalms 19:7b states, "The testimony of the LORD is sure, making wise the simple."

- **Grows us spiritually**

We will become strong and mature as we study God's Word. Psalms 1:2, 3 states, "But his delight is in the law of the LORD, and in His law he meditates day and night. He will be like a tree *firmly* planted by streams of water, which yields its fruit in its season and its leaf does not wither; and in whatever he does, he prospers."

Several years ago when working at IBM, I would do my devotions during my lunch break in my office. On one occasion before lunch I got into a serious argument with a coworker about the right technical approach on the project we worked on together. As I took my lunch break, I just happened to be reading in 2 Timothy. As I read, God got my attention. 2 Timothy 2:24-26 states, "The Lord's bond-servant must not be quarrelsome, but be kind to all, able to teach, patient when wronged, [25] with gentleness correcting those who are in opposition, if perhaps God may grant them repentance leading to the knowledge of the truth, [26] and they may come to their senses *and escape* from the snare of the devil, having been held captive by him to do his will." God got my attention in such a way that I claimed these verses as my life verses because they were so impactful.

- **Grows our faith**

We desire to be strong in our faith and not to be weak. We don't want the Lord to rebuke us as He did several times with His disciples.

- Mathew 17:19-20 "then the disciples came to Jesus privately and said, 'Why could we not drive it (demon) out?' And He said to them, 'Because of the littleness of your faith; for truly I say to you, if you have faith the size of a mustard seed, you will say to this mountain, Move from here to there, and it will move; and nothing will be impossible to you.'"
- Luke 12:28 "But if God so clothes the grass in the field, which is *alive* today and tomorrow is thrown into the furnace, how much more *will He clothe* you? You men of little faith!"

If we want to be strong in our faith we need to listen to God, and we can best do that through His Word. Romans 10:17 states, "So faith *comes* from hearing, and hearing by the word of Christ." As we listen, God will transform us by renewing our mind through His Word. As our faith grows our fears will subside. That's why the disciples were fearful about the storm and why Jesus said to them in Matthew 8:26, "Why are you afraid, you men of little faith?" Then He got up and rebuked the winds and the sea, and it became perfectly calm." If their faith was stronger, their fear would have been less. **Little faith a lot of fear and a lot of faith little fear.**

It helps us to understand the culture

- **So we can evaluate false teachers**

We live in a time where we as Christians do not know the Bible very well and because of that we are easily swayed by false teaching. A lot of teaching sounds good but in reality it is not Biblically sound. 2 Timothy 4:3 states, "For the time will come when they will not endure sound doctrine; but *wanting* to have their ears tickled, they will accumulate for themselves teachers in accordance to their own desires." I think this time **has** come, and most churches have abandoned sound doctrine, because that's not what people want to hear. Therefore, we need to be like the Bereans and continually check our teachers against the Scriptures to make sure they are correct. Acts 17:11 states, "Now these (Bereans) were more noble-minded than those in Thessalonica, for they received the word with great eagerness, **examining** the Scriptures daily *to see* whether these things were so."

- **Defeat the Enemy**

Most of the time, we forget that we are in the middle of a spiritual battle. We get caught up in the day to day struggles of life and forget the enemy wants to destroy us and our families. 1 Peter 5:8b states, "Your adversary, the devil, prowls around like a roaring lion, seeking someone to devour." We need a weapon strong enough to defeat this lion. According to Paul from the letter to Ephesians, that weapon is "the sword of the Spirit, which is the Word of God." (Ephesians 6:17b) Jesus said to Peter that Satan desired to sift him like wheat, and he wants to do the same with us. When the enemy tried to defeat Christ in the wilderness,

Jesus responded to each approach of the devil with the Word of God. Matthew 4:3, 4 states, "and the tempter came and said to Him, 'If You are the Son of God, command that these stones become bread.' But He answered and said, 'It is written, 'MAN SHALL NOT LIVE ON BREAD ALONE, BUT ON EVERY WORD THAT PROCEEDS OUT OF THE MOUTH OF GOD.'" If Jesus used the Word of God to defeat the enemy, we need to understand it enough so we can do likewise.

So we can understand the current times

- **Time of opportunity**

The days in which we live are filled with evil and tremendous moral decline. We have gone away from what's right and wrong as God has defined it. There is more violence and worldwide persecution of Christians. Our families are struggling. Our leaders are misled. But instead of viewing our present time with despair we should view it as an opportunity. Ephesians 5:16 states, "Make the most of every opportunity in these evil days. " (NLT) This is a tremendous time of opportunity to share the gospel and point people to God. The security of money and physical wellbeing is fleeting. The only place to find peace and security is in Christ.

- **Time of prophecy fulfillment**

The middle-east has the world's attention just like God said it would. To witness in our lifetime the regathering of the Jews in Israel is something miraculous. God has promised throughout scripture that the Jews would be scattered and brought back to the land He gave them, and we are witnessing that today. Isaiah 43:5-6 states do not fear, for I am with you; I will bring your (Israel's) offspring from the east, and gather you from the west.[6] "I will say to the north, 'Give *them* up!' and to the south, 'Do not hold *them* back.' bring My sons from afar and My daughters from the ends of the earth.

- **Maybe a time close to Christ's return**

John in the book of Revelation states "the time is near." (Rev 1:3b) He is referring to the return of Christ. We know we are in that era of His return but it may be a lot closer than we think. We know that Christ will return like a thief in the night. (1 Thessalonians 5:2) When no one is looking or watching. As we see the world and America continue to turn away from God and not looking for Christ's return, this could mean that the time is getting close. We know that prior to His return there will be famines and earthquakes. As we see more natural disasters greater than we have ever seen, this could be an indicator that we are getting close. Also, we know that when Christ returns He will come back to save His people the Jews. Today, we see a world that is growing stronger in opposition to Israel, and this could be an indicator that we are getting close. Just think maybe we or our children or grandchildren could be living when Christ returns. How great is that!

Luke 6:40 "A pupil is not above his teacher; but everyone, after he has been fully trained, will be like his teacher."

2 Timothy 2:2 "The things which you have heard from me in the presence of many witnesses, entrust these to faithful men who will be able to teach others also."

So we can learn and teach others

- **Be teachers**

As we learn the truths of scripture, God doesn't ask us to keep it to ourselves but to be willing to teach others so that they can be teachers. Hebrews 5:12 states, "For though by this time you ought to be teachers, you have need again for someone to teach you the elementary principles of the oracles of God, and you have come to need milk and not solid food." So, we need to learn and grow in our knowledge of the scriptures in order to be good teachers.

- **Be rewarded**

If we obey what we learn, we will also be rewarded. Proverbs 13:3b states, "The one who despises the word will be in debt to it, but the one who fears the commandment will be rewarded." And Psalms 19:9b-11 states, "The judgments of the LORD are true; they are righteous altogether.[10] They are more desirable than gold, yes, than much fine gold;
sweeter also than honey and the drippings of the honeycomb.[11] Moreover, by them Your servant is warned; In keeping them there is great reward."

- **Be counselors**

The word of God can make us competent counselors just like it did for Moses. Exodus 18:16 states, "when they (Jews) have a dispute, it comes to me (Moses), and I judge between a man and his neighbor and make known the statutes of God and His laws." Moses counseled and judged by using God's Word. We can also be good counselors just as Paul said of the Roman believers. Romans 15:14 states, "I myself (Paul) am convinced, my brothers and sisters, that you yourselves are full of goodness, filled with **knowledge** and **competent** to instruct one another." (NIV)

Challenge

My challenge to you is to step up your Bible study. If you are slack in attending a good Bible teaching church, become faithful. If you just attend church, get involved in a small Bible study group. If you are in a Bible study group, take a class that requires work to dig deeper, such as Precepts, or through a Bible college or Seminary. Also, look for opportunities to teach. The teacher always learns more than the student. **Let's get serious about our study of God's**

Word. Let us be like Ezra, "For Ezra had set his heart to **study** the law of the Lord and to **practice** it, and to **teach** His statutes and ordinances in Israel." (Ezra 7:10)

ARE WE USING OUR TIME WISELY?

Chapter 12

By Serving Others

Ephesians 2:10 (TLB) " It is God himself who has made us what we are and given us new lives from Christ Jesus; and long ages ago he planned that we should spend these lives in helping others."

GOD CALLS US TO SERVE OTHERS

God calls us to a life of service. Rick Warren says, "God calls you to a service far beyond anything you could ever imagine. You were put on Earth to make a contribution." Rick also says that "God wants you to give something back." In Ephesians 2:10b Paul states, "In our union with Christ Jesus He has created us for a life of good deeds, which He has already prepared for us to do."(TEV) Whenever we serve others, we are actually serving God. Matthew 25:40b states "Truly I say to you, to the extent that you did it to one of these brothers of Mine, *even* the least *of them*, you did it to Me." Billy Graham says, "The highest form of worship is the worship of unselfish Christian service. The greatest form of praise is the sound of consecrated feet seeking out the lost and helpless." Just as Jesus came to serve us and was an example to us so we then should serve others. Our love should overflow into service. In Galatians Paul states, "But through love serve one another," because "you shall love your neighbor as yourself." At this stage in our lives we should be an example to others. We should serve others both in the community as well as in the church.

In the community

In chapter two, I talked about our value to society. One of the ways in which we are valuable is through our volunteer service. As I said, older adults who volunteer typically volunteer more hours in a year than other age groups. In fact you are never too old to volunteer. Some examples recently posted by GreaterGoodness talk about older volunteers.

- **The 87-year-old EMT**

At 87 years young, Edna Mitchell is defying the stereotypes of aging by serving her community as Maine's oldest emergency medical technician. She began volunteering with the Liberty, Maine fire department in 1978. At a time in her life when most people consider retirement and slowing down, she dedicated her life to helping her neighbors, according to LittleThings.com. In 37 years of service, Mitchell has ensured that laboring moms get to the hospital in time and has assisted in heroic efforts to rescue vehicle accident victims. Mitchell has clearly inspired younger generations: two of her granddaughters and one great-granddaughter also serve the community as EMTs.

- **Giving Back in Her 90s**

Ana Ochoa of Omaha, NE, logs more than 1,000 hours of volunteer work each year. A Cuban immigrant, the 92-year-old created a successful career for herself in the banking industry. After her second retirement, she decided to spend time giving back to her community. Ochoa volunteers as an administrative assistant in a senior center, where she has served for 15 years. She also performs hostess duties at a local cancer center and provides translation services for hospice patients.

- **Comforting Hospice Patients**

Texas resident Ernest Bradbury felt a void in his life after his beloved wife passed away. He chose to deal with his pain by showing love and compassion to other dying patients. At 78 years old, Bradbury has spent the last 11 years of his life bringing joy into the lives of the terminally ill. The Lubbock, Texas community has recognized his efforts, as is detailed in SaluteToSeniorService.com. His efforts also assist the families of these patients, allowing them time to run errands or just have some valuable time to themselves. Bradbury says that he understands the loneliness that many senior citizens feel, especially after the loss of a spouse. He believes that volunteering has helped him cope and values the time he spends with his hospice patients.

- **Bringing Her Skills to the Community**

Retired oncology nurse Sandra Campbell uses her experience to bring emotional and financial support to oncology patients in the community of North Jackson, OH. The 71-year-old has spent the last five years providing hospice services to terminal cancer patients. She also makes quilts and donates them to the Oncology Fund for Outpatients. The Fund then sells the quilts, with the proceeds going to assist cancer patients with various expenses, such as groceries and medications. Four years ago, Campbell began visiting a hospice patient in her nineties. She provided companionship, as well as one of her handmade quilts, and shared in the woman's steady improvement. Though the patient has since been discharged from hospice care, Campbell continues to provide her with encouragement and care.

- **World War II Veteran Gives Back in Multiple Ways**

World War II veteran Don Buck serves his community in Las Cruces, NM through a variety of organizations. At 85 years old, he volunteers with his local Rotary Club and works as a Goodwill ambassador. He says that he did not want to sit around being unproductive and sees volunteering as a reason to get up each morning. Even as he cared for his own dying wife, Buck solicited the help of a professional caregiver so that he could continue his service to the community.

Senior citizens do provide valuable services to their communities. "No one is useless in this world who lightens the burdens of another." - Charles Dickens

In the Church

God calls us even more specifically to serve the body of Christ. Actually, He gives to us specific gifts in order to do just that. The spiritual gifts as listed in Ephesians 4, 1 Corinthians 12, and Romans 12 are divided into two basic categories of speaking and serving. So God gives a set of gifts for the sole purpose of serving others in the body. Ephesians 4:12 states these gifts are given "for the equipping of the saints for the work of service, to the building up the body of Christ." Some of the gifts specifically slated for serving are: leadership, helps, administration, mercy, service, giving, and possibly pastor. In a way the speaking gifts like teaching, exhortation, and evangelism (which I will cover later) also serve others. So God has gifted us to serve because it is important. 1 Peter 4:10 states, "As each one has received a special gift, employ it in serving one another as good stewards of the manifold grace of God."

In an article by Amy Hanson titled "Creating New Opportunities for Older Adults to Serve," she talks about Bobbi Baxter. "Bobbi always wanted to go on a mission trip, but didn't have the opportunity until she was 80 years old. While other retired women might be baking cookies or watching television, Bobbi joined this Second Half Ministries team from Northshore Baptist Church on a short-term mission trip to Nicaragua. She is not the only older adult who has invested time and energy in the lives of the poverty stricken people of that country. In fact, 45 to 50 percent of all the volunteers from Northshore who do short-term mission work in Nicaragua are 50 years of age or older."

In the same article Amy states six ways churches are creating new opportunities for service among older adults.

1. Making an intentional commitment to emphasize service for older adults.
2. Allowing many different starting points for new ministry.
3. Finding age-appropriate means of evangelism.
4. Serving on international teams and reaching out to a variety of generations.
5. Finding creative ways to integrate older adults into the community.
6. Partnering with other churches to utilize retirees.

Amy also states that "creating an atmosphere within an older adult ministry where service is an expected and normal thing does not automatically happen. Some churches have neglected to see their older adults as valuable resources full of life experience and wisdom, and instead they have bought into the world's lie that once someone reaches a particular age they should 'slow down' and 'let the younger people take over.' It takes effort and in some cases a shift in attitude to build an outwardly focused older adult ministry."

Some churches and parachurch organizations actually target senior adults for serving or volunteering opportunities. What a great idea! We should be serving. We have the time, and we are gifted for it, so why not target us? I still believe the greatest untapped resource for the church in modern America is the senior adults and this is one way to utilize that resource. If your church doesn't target senior adults to volunteer, perhaps you could be the senior adult volunteer coordinator. ☺ Just a thought.

Galatians 5:13b "But through love serve one another."

WE BENEFIT FROM SERVING OTHERS

Luke 6:38 states, "Give and it will be given to you. They will pour into your lap a good measure—pressed down, shaken together, *and* running over. For by your standard of measure it will be measured to you in return." Not that this should be our motivation, but we do gain a lot of benefit from serving others. An article titled "Volunteering and its Surprising Benefits" published by HelpGuide gives some ways that helping others can help us.

- **Volunteering connects you to others**

The article states that unpaid volunteers are often the glue that holds a community together. It says that volunteering allows you to connect to your community and make it a better place. Your volunteering helps you make new friends, expand your network, and boost your social skills.

- **Volunteering is good for your mind and body**

It states that volunteering; increases self-confidence, provides a sense of purpose, combats depression, and helps you stay physically healthy. Those who volunteer have a lower mortality rate. Even people with physical disabilities find improvement after volunteering.

Dr. Bill Thomas experiment – posted on Facebook and taken from a Washington Post article

> Dr. Bill Thomas, a Harvard-trained physician and a 2015 Next Avenue Influencer in Aging, has a message he'd like to share with the world: Growing older is a good thing.
>
> A recent Washington Post story highlighted Thomas's crusade to change attitudes about aging and encourage people to think of "post-adulthood" as a time of enrichment. "Thomas believes that Americans have bought so willingly into the idea of aging as something to be feared that it has become

a self-fulfilling prophecy leading to isolation, loneliness, and lack of autonomy," the article stated.

In 1991, Thomas became the medical director of a nursing home in upstate New York. He found the place, as the Post put it, "depressing, and a repository for old people whose minds and bodies seemed dull and dispirited."

So, what did Thomas do? The Washington Post explains:

[Dr. Thomas] decided to transform the nursing home. Based on a hunch, he persuaded his staff to stock the facility with two dogs, four cats, several hens and rabbits, and 100 parakeets, along with hundreds of plants, a vegetable and flower garden, and a day-care site for staffers' kids.

All those animals in a nursing home broke state law, but for Thomas and his staff, it was a revelation. Caring for the plants and animals restored residents' spirits and autonomy; many started dressing themselves, leaving their rooms and eating again. The number of prescriptions fell to half of that of a control nursing home, particularly for drugs that treat agitation. Medication costs plummeted, and so did the death rate.

He named the approach the Eden Alternative — based on the idea that a nursing home should be less like a hospital and more like a garden — and it was replicated in hundreds of institutions in Canada, Europe, Japan and Australia as well as in all 50 U.S. states (the animal restriction in New York was voted down).

As the residents served each other by caring for the animals and the gardens, they improved their own life.

- **Volunteering brings fun and fulfillment to your life**

They say that volunteering is fun and is an easy way to expand your personal interests and passions. So find the right place to volunteer that fits those passions and interests. Some places they suggest to find volunteer opportunities are:

- Community theaters, museums, and monuments
- Libraries and senior centers
- Service organizations
- Local animal shelters and rescue organizations

Find the right volunteer opportunity that works well for you, and this can be a way of connecting to others for the purpose of sharing the gospel.

WE SHOULD SERVE OTHERS FOR THE PURPOSE OF SHARING THE GOSPEL

In 1 Corinthians 9:19 Paul states, "For though I am free from all, I have made myself a servant to all, that I might win more of them." (ESV) In this day and age, building relationships by connecting to others through service or community activities in order to have spiritual conversations is very important. Because of its importance, I have committed the next chapter (13) to discuss it.

WE SHOULD BE CAREFUL WHEN WE SERVE

There can be several benefits from serving others. However, we should not be motivated by what we think we will receive but by love and commitment for those we serve. If we serve to be noticed by others and to receive applause, our rewards will be limited. Matthew 6:1-3 states, "Beware of practicing your righteousness before men to be noticed by them; otherwise you have no reward with your Father who is in heaven.[2] "So when you give to the poor, do not sound a trumpet before you, as the hypocrites do in the synagogues and in the streets, so that they may be honored by men. Truly I say to you, they have their reward in full. ³ But when you give to the poor, do not let your left hand know what your right hand is doing. "We should be so motivated that we shouldn't be patting ourselves on the back with one hand while serving with the other. Don't be looking around for praise, but serve truly esteeming others more important than ourselves. Philippians 2:3-7 states, "³ Do nothing from selfishness or empty conceit, but with humility of mind regard one another as more important than yourselves; ⁴ do not merely look out for your own personal interests, but also for the interests of others. ⁵ Have this attitude in yourselves which was also in Christ Jesus, ⁶ who, although He existed in the form of God, did not regard equality with God a thing to be grasped, ⁷ but emptied Himself, taking the form of a bond-servant, and being made in the likeness of men. In an article posted by David Peach about "Putting Others before Yourself," he gives some tips on how to do this.

Be Compassionate

One of the many attributes that characterizes Christ is His compassion. Of course He was God, but He was also a man with a desire to serve others because of His love for them. Jesus Christ is our example.

We can ask the Lord to develop compassion in our lives. He said to His followers that those who are truly His disciples will show love to one another. It is probably easier to love fellow Christians than those who do not know our Father, but the example that Christ gave was to love other people regardless of their spiritual condition.

Be Empathetic

Consider the needs of those around you. Try to put yourself in their situation and treat them as you would like to be treated. We call this the Golden Rule and it is found in Matthew 7:12, "In everything, therefore, treat people the same way you want them to treat you, for this is the Law and the Prophets."

We often talk about putting ourselves in someone else's shoes. That is a good way to think of empathy. When you are having trouble getting along with, or helping, someone else, try to picture yourself in the same condition or position they are in. How would you like people to treat you? Treat them the same way and you will become more empathetic to their needs.

Develop a Servant's Heart

You have to yield to Him so that He can work in your life.

Find ways to serve others. This is the best way to develop a servant's heart. Putting others before yourself is easier when you are serving them. But just because someone is in a serving position does not mean that they are serving with the right attitude. Maybe you have met people who are involved in a service industry who don't enjoy serving others. Even people in compassionate sounding jobs (working at a homeless shelter or working as a nurse for example) can have the wrong attitude about the people they are serving.

Develop a servant's heart and attitude. This is the work of the Holy Spirit. You have to yield to Him so that He can work in your life.

Realize That People Think Differently

One of the reasons we find it hard to put others before ourselves is that often people think differently than we do. If my family thought exactly the same way I did then we might have fewer problems, but life would sure be boring. We like the diversity of thought that different people bring to a group. However, it can also be the source of friction. Try to learn to see and understand things from the other person's perspective.

Don't try to force everyone into your way of thinking. That is a sign that you are thinking more of yourself than you are of them.

Consider Their Welfare More Important Than Your Desires

Jesus Christ came to earth for the good of mankind. While we are trying to be compassionate and more empathetic, we should see what others need. This does not mean that we give them anything and everything they want nor allow others to walk all over us. It means that we try to find out their true needs, and try to help them even if it is uncomfortable for us.

So, be careful but serve!

Challenge

God calls us to serve others, and we can receive great benefits from doing that. While serving, we should look for opportunities to build relationships in order to have spiritual conversations. Think about an area where you can serve, or as I said before, be the older adult volunteer coordinator for your church.

"Those who are the happiest are those who do the most for others" Booker T. Washington

"Self-improvement comes mainly from trying to help others" – John Templeton

ARE WE USING OUR TIME WISELY?

Chapter 13

By Witnessing

2 Timothy 4:5 "But you, be sober in all things, endure hardship, do the work of an evangelist, fulfill your ministry."

RELATIONAL EVANGELISM

If you have been a Christian for any length of time, you have been exposed to various evangelistic strategies. You feel as if you have heard it all, and you may be asking yourself an important question: Why would I need to read this chapter on evangelism? My question to you is this: How is your current evangelistic strategy working? Have the evangelistic books you have read or witnessing classes you have taken improved your personal evangelism? Has the Bible changed? Has God's great plan of salvation changed? **Absolutely not!** However, your evangelistic mindset may need to change in order for you to be a more successful "fisher of men."
We all desire to be evangelistic. As believers, we want to be obedient to Christ's "Great Commission", but we rarely engage in spiritual conversations with unbelievers. When we do, the conversations tend to be forced and awkward. So, how can we become more effective evangelists in today's culture and have spiritual conversations that are not awkward?

Right Approach
Today, we need an evangelistic strategy that fits the culture.

A 2007 Barna survey revealed a changing atmosphere in our culture.

- In the mid-nineties, the vast majority of Americans outside of the Christian faith felt favorably towards Christian's role in society.
- Today 91% of American Evangelicals believe that Americans are becoming more hostile and negative toward Christianity

- Currently, only 16% of 16-29 year old non-Christians express a favorable view toward Christians in general and only 3% express a favorable view toward evangelical Christians
- Non-Christians view Christians as judgmental (87%), hypocritical (85%), and old fashioned (78%)

The most disturbing thing about this data is that these perceptions of non-Christians toward Christians are rooted in specific stories of interactions with Christians. Today, we must be **Relational Evangelists.** Relationship building can simply be a conversation on an airplane or developing an ongoing friendship with a neighbor. The key is that in most evangelistic encounters today we must develop a relationship first in order to "earn" the privilege of impacting people spiritually.

We live at a time when strong relationships are not normal. Today, close relationships are limited or non-existent. Max Lucado said in his book *Out Live Your Life,* "Our society is set up for isolation. We wear our earbuds when we exercise. We communicate via e-mail and text messages. We enter and exit our houses with gates and garage-door openers. Our mantra: I leave you alone. You leave me alone. Yet God wants his people to be an exception."

A 2008 Barna survey found that:

- Atheists and agnostics were more likely to cite their workplace as their top social network.
- Christians in general were evenly divided with 1/5th identifying work, 1/5th identifying their church, and 1/5th listing their friends as their primary social network.
- 74% of all evangelicals said their church was their social network

From this summary, we can see that only 20% of Christians in general, claim their church as their primary social network. But 74% of more committed Christians claim the church. So, as we become more committed in our faith, we actually become more isolated from unbelievers. Therefore, if we are to reach out to those who need to hear the good news of the Gospel, we must be proactive in developing relationships with them.

So what is Relational Evangelism?

All of our relationships are at different levels. The key is that relationships are progressive. As we get closer to someone, the opportunities for effective spiritual conversations increase in number and depth. We must recognize that the relationship model has a target: to bring people into the family of God. The concentric rings in the figure below represent the levels of interpersonal relationship between the believer and the unbeliever. As we approach the center, we reach the target.

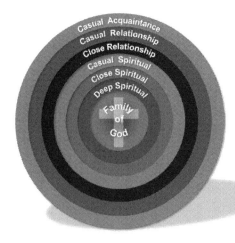

1. **Casual Acquaintance**
2. **Casual Relationship**
3. **Close Relationship**
4. **Casual Spiritual Relationship**
5. **Close Spiritual Relationship**
6. **Deep Spiritual Relationship**
7. **Family of God Relationship**

1 - 3 Secular Relationship Circles

4 - 6 Spiritual Relationship Circles

Secular Relationship Circles

In this relationship model, the three outer circles represent three secular relationship levels. These are relationships that focus on getting to learn general information about the person as the precursor to discovering the person's spiritual condition. No spiritual conversations take place at these levels. The outer circle is defined as a Casual Acquaintance. This is someone who lives in the same community, shops at the same grocery store, or works in the same building. We recognize those folks, but we really don't know anything about them.

The next inner secular circle is defined as a Casual Relationship. These are people we actually know. We know their names and maybe something about their family, but that's about it. In today's environment, it could be a next door neighbor. We see them come and go but don't know much about them. The final secular relationship is defined as a Close Relationship. At this point, we still have not had a spiritual conversation with them, but we know where they work, what they enjoy (golf?), and something about their family. Perhaps, we had them over for a barbecue or went out with them in a neighborhood dine out group. We have been involved with them in some smaller group activity, and through that activity we are getting to know them better. All these are still secular relationships, and we desire to move closer in order to have a spiritual conversation with them.

Spiritual Relationship Circles

The next three circles represent spiritual relationships. These are relationships where we are having some form of spiritual conversation with them. The outermost spiritual relationship is defined as a Casual Spiritual Relationship. This is a relationship in which we break the ice, spiritually. We have made the transition from the weather to perhaps where they go to church or to ask whether they believe in a divine creator. So we have started, but it's early.

The second inner spiritual circle is defined as Close Spiritual Relationship. At this point, we are still getting spiritual information about them. By now, we know their church background and church attendance habits. We know some of their childhood stories, why they do or don't attend a church, and about how they were raised. We have invited them to church related activities, and although they have come to some, we are still not sure of their spiritual condition. The final spiritual circle is defined as Deep Spiritual Relationship. At this stage, spiritual conversations are commonplace. We know where they are spiritually, and we are sharing the gospel with them in an ongoing manner when we have opportunity.

Family of God Circle

We see them moving closer to God and view it as just a matter of time until they take that step of faith. The final circle is defined as the Family of God Circle. They have taken the step to believe in Christ. Now your relationship with them is changed forever. This is our bull's eye that keeps us on track throughout all of the other relationship circles or levels.

Not every relationship will start at the outer most circle and end with them accepting Christ. Some relationships will start out there but get stalled or stop within one of the circles. Some will quickly go to the spiritual relationship level, but others will take a long time.

We can have many relationships at a time that are likely to be at different levels. In all cases it's important that we prayerfully seek God's help to move them move closer to Him. We will not always get the privilege to reap what we sow, but we might also be able to reap what others have sown. God usually works in several ways through several different people. John 4:37b - 38 says, "One sows and another reaps. I sent you to reap that for which you have not labored; others have labored and you have entered into their labor."

Get out there!

The first and most important step in building any relationship is to meet them where they are. Mark 1:17 states, and Jesus said to them "Follow me and I will make you become fishers of men." A successful fisherman knows how to find the fish. He knows where they are at a specific time of the day. He knows when they go to a shady area to escape from the sun and when they go to another area to feed. So, just as a fisherman finds the fish, we must be involved with unbelievers in places where they live and work. This doesn't mean we go to places or participate in activities that God wouldn't like, but where He approves we **must** go.

Get Involved!

Become involved in non-church activities and organizations. Joe Aldrich in his book *Life Style Evangelism* said that his neighbors were tennis players, so he became a tennis player, and two neighbors came to Christ. This is going to where the fish are. So as you develop relationships through activities, you must become involved in their lives. Paul said in I Corinthians 9:22, "To the weak I became weak that I might win the weak; I have become all things to all men, so that I may by all means save some." Paul became like those he was trying to reach without hurting his testimony. He wanted them to be comfortable around him, and he did not want to offend them in order to build relationships.

Chapter 12 on Serving gives you a lot of ideas on how to get involved in order to build relationships. Maybe, you could start an activity such as a monthly game night or card club. Others have started or plugged into biking and walking groups. Do you have a pet? Dog owners love to talk about their dogs while walking them. Take a watercolor class at a local community college or activity center. Audition for a community theatre group. Feel uncomfortable going it alone? Bring a Christian friend along, but

have the same goal: to make new friends. Whatever activity you get involved in get there early and leave late. The time before and after the activity is important in building relationships.
Now we can develop some relationships, but how do we get closer to them in order to have spiritual conversations?

Building Close Relationships

At this point, we have established several casual relationships, but we need to grow closer to some of them so that we can have more personal conversations in order to move from just secular to spiritual discussions. To do this, we should go from group activities to one-on-one or two-on-two activities, because people are more open about themselves in a smaller group. For me, I would look for opportunities to golf with a smaller, more regular set of guys. I actually finished my basement and put in a putting green and driving net so that I could invite others over to use them. I think this was the main reason, but it has improved my putting. ☺ In her chorale group, Carol started a birthday card ministry in which she would send cards to women in the chorale or in the neighborhood. Through this simple act of kindness, she touched hearts, and the women were truly grateful.

Look For Opportunities

We must be always on the lookout for opportunities to develop closer relationships through one-on-one or small group activities. One way to do this is to recognize where God is at work and get involved. An opportunity came for me after a normal summer interclub golf match. It was especially hot that day, but everything seemingly went okay. We didn't have any cases of heat exhaustion as we were very careful. But on the following day one of the golfers got up in the morning and couldn't see. From his perspective, he was totally blind. As captain, I felt the responsibility and opportunity to move closer. I immediately visited him and offered my prayers. I also asked other golfers to pray. After going to a doctor, he realized that only one eye was damaged, but it also affected the sight in the good eye. So by patching the bad eye, he could see, and over the next of several months, the damaged eye healed to the point of being almost normal. So through the damaged eye, a close relationship got started and eventually led to his trusting Christ as his personal savior.

Love Them

Taking this step in going beyond a secular and casual relationship takes love and commitment. We must truly be interested in them, their struggles, their successes, and their lives. This is where we must "Love your neighbor as yourself" (Leviticus 19:18).

We live in Virginia, and the last couple of winters we have had an abundance of snow. At the time of one of these snowfalls, I was preparing a Sunday school lesson on relational evangelism, so the Great Commandment was on my heart as I was outside shoveling snow. I grew up in Western Pennsylvania, and we also lived in upstate New York for five years, so snow had been a part of our lives. Since the winters were longer there, we were very careful in our snow shoveling techniques. I would push and throw the snow on the downwind side, always shovel to the edges to let the sun clear off the remaining snow, shovel all sidewalks, and clear off a place in front of the mailbox for the mailperson. I had completed our home area and proceeded to go to our neighbors' home. They were several years older than we were and not able to shovel.

As I started, I was cold and tired, so I attempted to cut corners where I could. They had a two car garage but only had one car, so my reasoning was to only clear one side of the driveway. Also, I thought they didn't need to use their sidewalk. They could just go through the garage and down the driveway to get the mail. While shoveling, God reminded me of that little verse found in Mark 12, The Great Commandment. So in my mind I questioned, "What does it really mean to love your neighbor as yourself?" As God spoke to me in this situation, I understood that He clearly doesn't mean for me to cut corners on my neighbor's snow. I should actually shovel my neighbor's driveway and sidewalk in the same way that I would do my own. I cleared everything to the edges, the way a true New Yorker would do.

Serve Them

Mark Mittleberg said, "Our message of love has much more impact when preceded by our acts of love." Removing snow, sending birthday cards, getting their mail, buying magazines, and watching their kids are acts of love that can open a door to the greatest message of love. The serving style as defined by Mark and Lee is about being others-oriented, working behind the scenes, and showing patience.

We have been building close relationships by looking for opportunities where God is already at work and serving in them with a loving heart. Now we are ready to cross the threshold of secular relationships. We have gotten close through secular activities, and now we must see if our friends are open to spiritual conversations.

Building Casual Spiritual Relationships

We have developed a secular relationship through group and one-on-one activities, but we haven't yet had any spiritual conversations with our new friends. This is where most people get stalled. We are convinced that we can witness by our lifestyle, which is important, but in order to have a spiritual conversation, we must say something. We must take that first step and turn a natural or normal conversation into a spiritual one. Before we do this, we need some proper preparation.

This proper preparation involves two parts, prayer and place. We must be praying for God to soften their hearts and enable them to be open to discuss where they are spiritually. Develop an evangelical prayer list. Make this a list of people who need Christ and with whom you have a relationship. Then pray for them daily. Always be open to add new people to the list. Pray specifically for the next step in the relationship process. If it's to start a spiritual conversation, pray for wisdom and the right words, so that they would be receptive and that they would respond positively.

The second part in preparation is to have a place. We must create a safe environment where you can find out where they are spiritually. So, move to a more conversational environment by continuing the one-on-one meetings. This could be a deliberate meeting such as a breakfast or dinner, or could be as simple as driving to play golf or racquetball. They must be free to speak openly. They rarely will be open in front of others, so one-on-one is important.

Questioning

Now that they are prayed up, and we have a place; we must be ready to start a spiritual conversation by asking a question. We need to have at least one question ready. My most used question is "Do you attend church?" or "Are you a church goer?" This is usually non-threatening, and yet can give you a lot of insight as to where they are spiritually.

Have one question ready that can jump-start a spiritual conversation, but also be ready for other more natural or bridge transitions to spiritual conversations.

Bridging

On one occasion, we were out to dinner with our neighbors. Our discussion centered on medical issues and operations because our neighbor was soon to go through a major surgery and was very concerned. I simply stated that I was presently reading a book on Heaven by Randy Alcorn and that when we get to heaven we will receive a new body without the need for surgery and doctors. From this opening, I was able to explain the gospel message completely.

Bridging to spiritual conversations can take some planning. Think of a statement or comment that would be a good transition statement for you. But also be ready to bridge from the conversation or situation at hand.

Invite to church related activities

After you have broken the ice with a spiritual conversation, a good follow-up would be to invite them to a church related event. As I stated in chapter 3, 25% of unchurched adults would probably come to church if a friend invited them. Sometimes when our church has a ticketed event, we simply buy some extra tickets and pray for the "friend" we should invite. On one occasion, we did this for our Christmas program and invited a neighborhood couple. The guy was blown away with the brass band that performed because he used to play in a brass band. From that invitation, he loved our church and became a faithful attendee.

By inviting a friend to a church event, you could be helping someone come back to church. A 2011 Barna survey stated that adult church attendance has dropped by 11% for women and 6% for men over the last twenty years.

We must be "bridgers" and "inviters" to impact lives. As we bridge and invite, we attempt to move them closer and to move from a casual spiritual relationship to a close spiritual relationship.

Building Close Spiritual Relationships

We have progressed in our relationship. Now we know some of their spiritual background. We understand what they believe, and we may even know what some of their objections are to the

Christian faith. This is where we start. We must begin at the point where they are spiritually. Paul started from creation for pagans and from the Old Testament for Jews. Before we attempt to move them closer to Christ, we should discuss with them the areas where we agree. By first having discussions on topics on which we agree, we are making our new friends comfortable in having spiritual discussions, which makes the next step in the process easier.

I golf with a person of the Muslim faith, and he is very comfortable discussing spiritual issues with me. We first started at creation with Adam and Eve. We now discuss areas of difference, but it's not argumentative, and we maintain a good relationship.

Relational Seeker Small Groups

Continue the one-on-ones and go deeper with your spiritual conversations. As you develop these relationships, you might consider starting a Relational Seeker Small Group. This is a group Bible study around a specific activity. It must be convenient and Bible light. We have a men's golf outing/league every Monday during the summer and get sometimes 60-70 men in our community out for golf. I started a 15 minute pre-golf Bible study before our shotgun start. We normally start at 9:00am, so I would have the Bible study from 8:15am – 8:30am in the office of our club pro. At first, no one would come, but eventually it grew to 10-12 guys.

Think about what you could do around your activity. Perhaps with a walking or biking group, you could have a small Bible study before or after you walk or ride.

At this point in your relationship you will get more questions, and you will have fewer answers. That is good because witnessing will cause you to study. Paul stated in II Timothy 2:15, "Study to show thyself approved unto God, a workman that needeth not to be ashamed, rightly dividing the word of truth." (KJV)

Be diligent and study to be more effective, but never be argumentative. We can discuss and to some degree debate but never argue. Now our relationship is getting closer, and the spiritual discussions are getting deeper. Next let's look at building a deep spiritual relationship.

Building Deep Spiritual Relationships

We have had several spiritual discussions. Perhaps we have discussed some hard issues like "Why is there evil in the world?" or "Why does God allow us to suffer?" They are intellectually interested, but because of their religious background or lack of religious background they don't understand the concept of having a personal relationship with God. We need to help them experience God on a personal level not just an intellectual level. As they begin to experience God personally, and you share with them some of your experiences with God, your relationship with them will grow deeper.

Now is a good time to challenge them to SEEK God. II Chronicles 15:2b states, "And if you seek Him, He will let you find Him; but if you forsake Him, He will forsake you." Our pastor Lon Solomon tells his story about asking God for a Bible to read. He was broke and couldn't afford a Bible, but he told God if He would supply the Bible, Lon would read it. God supplied a Bible through a street evangelist. Lon read it and eventually put his faith in Christ.

When you challenge them, be careful to tell them to seek God with a humble heart and be fully open to God. We can't approach God with pride or arrogance and expect Him to respond, so humility is important. Challenge them to seek God, and maintain an environment with them where spiritual conversations are commonplace. Our pastor Lon says, "Keep a consistent verbal witness to them, but don't hound them all the time."

I had a coworker, Lonnie, with whom I had this type of relationship. I had several spiritual conversations with Lonnie, and we could talk freely. Our discussions were always friendly and relaxed, but Lonnie wasn't ready to take that step of faith. On a regular basis, not daily, I would simply say to Lonnie "are you ready to get saved today?" Lonnie would simply smile and say no, not today. He never got angry or said quit asking me. So I continued, until one day I asked the question, and he said yes. I was completely blown away. So I suggested we have lunch together. We bought some sandwiches and went to a local park where Lonnie put his faith in Christ. He then walked the walk. When his wife became ill with cancer, he was able to lead her to the Lord. So, keep spiritual conversations on going, not stressful, but natural and relaxed.

Challenge
This chapter was taken from my book "Relational Evangelism for Today." If you would like a copy, you can get it from Amazon or through the publisher Xulon Press. The book will discuss some tools you can use to lead someone to Christ. So, go out and build relationships in order to have spiritual conversations. This can be one of the most exciting and rewarding use of our time.

"Good works is giving to the poor and the helpless, but divine works is showing them their worth to the One who matters" Criss Jami

1 Corinthians 9:19b (ESV) "I have made myself a servant to all, that I might win more of them"

ARE WE HELPING THE YOUNGER?

Chapter 14

By Being a Good Example

Matthew 5:16 "Let your light shine before men in such a way that they may see your good works, and glorify your Father who is in heaven. "

If we are going to lead and influence younger generations, we **HAVE** to be a good example! We can't slack off and think no one is watching. Even if that was the case and no human is watching, God is watching. He is looking for godly men and women that He can use. I have stated before that I think we are the solution to our country's and our churches' problems. But I also think we **are** the problem. We have not been a good example and as a result those institutions are struggling. We have spent several chapters on how to grow spiritually and to be a good example. Please don't underestimate the importance of our example to others. **We should be a good example.**

Because God is our example

We all remember the "WWJD" (What Would Jesus Do?) bracelets and the challenge to live and do the things that Jesus as our example would do. Certainly, we can't do everything that Christ did as we do not have the knowledge or the power of God but as our perfect example we can strive to be like Him. Actually, that is the primary purpose of the Christian life, to be like Christ. John MacArthur states, "Spiritual living, the Christian life, is a process of pursuing Christ likeness... We must become more and more like Jesus Christ. Simply stated that is the Christian life"

John 13:13-15 "You call Me Teacher and Lord; and you are right, for *so* I am. [14] If I then, the Lord and the Teacher, washed your feet, you also ought to wash one another's feet. [15] For I gave you an **example,** that you also should do as I did to you."

Ephesians 5:1-2 "Therefore be **imitators** of God, as beloved children; [2] and walk in love, just as Christ also loved you and gave

Himself up for us, an offering and a sacrifice to God as a fragrant aroma."

1 Peter 2:21 "For you have been called for this purpose, since Christ also suffered for you, leaving you an **example** for you to follow in His steps,"

1 Timothy 1:16 "Yet for this reason I found mercy, so that in me as the foremost, Jesus Christ might demonstrate His perfect patience as an **example** for those who would believe in Him for eternal life."

In my men's community Tuesday night Bible study, we just finished the small group video series by Andy Stanley titled "Follow." Andy states that Jesus invites us to follow Him just as He did for the first century disciples. As John MacArthur says "the goal then of every Christian is to be like Christ. That is the goal. That is the thing we pursue…. It then becomes the life-long objective of every Christian to become more and more and more like Jesus Christ."

Because God gives us many examples in the Bible to follow

- **Noah** is one of the greatest examples of **obedience** in scripture. He built a boat where it had never rained and there wasn't any water. Humanly speaking that's far worse than building a boat in the basement and then realizing you can't get it out. He built the ark as God told him and warned his fellow men that divine judgment was coming. Genesis 6:22 states, "Thus Noah did; according to all that God had commanded him, so he did."
- **Abraham** is one of the greatest examples of **faith** in scripture. His faith grew throughout his life from the time when he was asked by God to go to a land he did not know and then later in his life he was asked to sacrifice his beloved son. As a result of his faith he was declared righteous by God. Genesis 15:6

states, "Then he (Abraham) believed in the LORD; and He (God) reckoned it to him as righteousness.
- **Joseph** is one of the greatest examples of **forgiveness** in scripture. Joseph was the favorite son of his father Jacob. He was envied by his brothers to the point where they were going to kill him but sold him into slavery instead. Then after imprisonment in Egypt, Joseph became the second in command of the strongest nation on the earth and had great authority and power. However, he never used his power to retaliate against his brothers but forgave them. Genesis 50:20 states, "As for you (his brothers), you meant evil against me, *but* God meant it for good in order to bring about this present result, to preserve many people alive."
- **Moses** is one of the greatest examples of **humility** in scripture. To become the deliverer of a whole nation and be God's agent to defeat one of the greatest nations on the earth would instill a sense of pride in most everyone. But, Moses maintained a sense of humility. When he was personally attacked or complained about by Aaron, and Miriam, he prayed for them. He also talked with God as a man talks to a friend. Instead of becoming proud, he was humble. Numbers 12:3 states "Now the man Moses was very humble, more than any man who was on the face of the earth."

These men gave us good, not perfect examples. When people talk about you, what kind of example would they say you are? Maybe not a fair question, but one you should think about as you seek to be a good example for others to follow.

Because God tells us to be a good example for others to follow

Paul instructed individuals to be good examples for others to follow. To Timothy he said "Let no one look down on your youthfulness, but *rather* in speech, conduct, love, faith *and* purity, show yourself an **example** of those who believe" (1 Timothy 4:12). To Titus he said, "In all things show yourself to be an **example** of good deeds, *with* purity in doctrine, dignified," (Titus 2:7). So, to Paul a good **example** is a big deal. Peter stressed to those in leadership the importance of being a good example. 1 Peter 5:3 states, "nor yet as lording it over those allotted to your charge, but proving to be **examples** to the flock."

Through Paul and Peter, God is speaking to us about the importance of a good example, as people do have a tendency to look more at what we do versus what we say, even though our speech is also an important example.

Because God gave us good personal examples to follow

God tells it's ok to imitate others who are godly examples. Hebrews 13:7 states, "Remember those who led you, who spoke the word of God to you; and considering the result of their conduct, imitate their faith." Before I came to Christ I was dating Carol. Her youth leader, Jim Quinn was a godly man, a big guy, and an x-football player. I had never played football but I loved to play baseball and started to play softball with her church group. I used to play short stop and because of my strong arm I could play deep and still throw runners out at first base. The first time Jim came to bat against me, I saw a large, heavy, and probably slow runner so I played deep and he proceeded to hit me a ground ball. I charged it as usual and looked up to throw him out only to see him flying past the bag. I never played him deep again. Jim befriended me, and I looked up to his godly example. I will look forward to seeing him again when I leave this earth.

As we imitate others who influenced us, we should encourage others to imitate us. I know this sounds boastful and arrogant, but if we want to influence others to follow Christ they must also see how we follow Christ, to help them in their walk. Paul was a humble, obedient, faithful Christ follower but he was not shy in encouraging others to follow his example. To the church at Thessalonica he said "not because we do not have the right *to this*, but in order to offer ourselves as a model for you, so that you would follow our example." (2 Thessalonians 3:9). To the church at Corinth he also said, "Therefore I exhort you, be imitators of me" (1 Corinthians 4:16). And to the Philippians, "Brethren, join in following my example, and observe those who walk according to the pattern you have in us" (Philippians 3:17).

One example in scripture that tells us people are watching comes from Romans chapter 14 and the passage about the weaker brother. Here, we see that one believer (the weaker) is watching very closely the other more mature believer. First, we see that he watches what we do. Romans 14:2 states, "One person has faith that he may eat all things, but he who is weak eats vegetables *only*." He also observes what we think, Romans 14:5a states, "One person regards one day above another, another regards every day *alike*." Because the weaker brother is watching us we need to be careful and "not put an obstacle or stumbling block in a brother's way" (Romans 14:13b). So, God says to be careful because you are an example, and even though what you are doing is ok, you might be causing a problem for a weaker believer.

This issue became apparent to me as I was told how guys watch closely how I behave on the golf course. Do I observe the complex rules of golf or do I bend them when I think no one is watching. Believe me people are watching a lot more than you think.

Several years ago, our daughter in law was having problems in her second pregnancy. Carol brought their older son back to our home in Virginia for a few weeks while our daughter in law was confined to bed. Zac was only around 2-3 years old and very observant. One day when Carol was driving and Zac was in the back seat a car pulled in front of them and Carol instinctively responded "dumb jerk." Zac picked up on this and when he returned to his parents he quickly showed them what grandma taught him while he was away. ☺ So people are watching, adults as well as children.

Because our example is fading

Previously, I stated that we are the solution to our country's problems, and I truly believe that. I also believe very strongly that we are also part of the problem. We have been influenced by the culture, and as a result, our moral values are fading. We are slipping away and so is our country. In an article titled "Older Americans' Moral Attitudes Changing" by Joy Wilde and Lydia Saad, they look at several specific areas where the moral values of older Americans have changed as shown through Gallup polls. They stated that moral acceptance has seen significant changes across all age groups in the last 15 years, but the greatest change has occurred among Americans aged 55 and older.

- **Gay Relations**

Overall, the acceptance of the gay and lesbian lifestyle has shown the greatest change between 2001 and 2013. The largest change in attitude being among older Americans which has increased by 25 percentage points.

- **Having a Baby Outside of Marriage**

The percentage of Americans who say it is morally acceptable to have a baby outside of marriage has gone from 45% to 60% between 2001 and 2013. Again, the largest change is in older adults going from 29% to 57%.

- **Premarital Sex**

Wilke and Saad state that "Americans aged 55 and older are largely responsible for the overall 10-point increase in moral acceptance of sex between unmarried men and women since 2001, from 53% to 63%. Among the older group, acceptance of premarital sex has increased by 22 points in 12 years, while the numbers have risen slightly among Americans younger than 55.

- **Divorce**

Older Americans are also driving the overall increase acceptance of divorce. The older Americans are 21 points more likely to find divorce acceptable in 2013 than they were in 2001.

So, clearly the moral attitudes of older Americans have been declining. Certainly, the influences of society's pressures through the media and leadership has been a large contributing factor, but our decline in holding on to Biblical truths is probably the main reason. We can see the decline in Biblical values in the younger generations and therefore can assume that the decline has been occurring in older adults as well. I could not find any surveys to support this over the last 15 years, but if I was a gambling man I would bet my house on it. (OK maybe I wouldn't) Three surveys commissioned by the American Bible Society and conducted by the Barna Research Group shows a decline in just two years. The surveys were done in 2013, 2014, and 2015 in answer to the question "Does the Bible have too little influence on society today?" The elders surveyed said yes by 63% in 2013, 61% in 2014 and 59% in 2015. My conclusion is that their opinion has dropped on the question of should the Bible have influence on our society. These three surveys were conducted with the same group of people. In 2013, elders surveyed were 67 and older. In 2014, they were 68 and older, and in 2015, they were 69 and older. I would assume if they were all conducted with the same age group, the results would even be greater.

I know this is shocking news. The moral decline in America is primarily a result of the older adults. The older still have an edge over the younger but they are changing rapidly. **Our example is fading and people are watching!** We need to turn the tide and determine to change back.

I think in order to keep from being unduly influenced by the society around us we need to be strongly influenced by God's Word. Only then can we truly discern right from wrong in a culture where we are continuing to be upside down. In a lot of places, it seems right is now wrong and what is wrong is right.

This just further emphasizes the fact that we need to be a strong and steady example. Just as the psalmist said in Psalms 1:2, 3, "But his delight is in the law of the LORD, and in His law he meditates day and night. He will be like a tree *firmly* planted by streams of water, which yields its fruit in its season and its leaf does not wither; and in whatever he does, he prospers." We will be like that tree firmly planted and still bear fruit and not be moved by the cultural influences around us.

1 Corinthians 11:1 "Be imitators of me, just as I also am of Christ."

STAND STRONG

In the next chapter I will discuss some ways we can fight back against the moral decline in our country.

ARE WE HELPING THE YOUNGER?

Chapter 15

By Attacking the Culture – Fighting Back

Proverbs 14:34 "Righteousness exalts a nation but sin is a disgrace to any people."

I was saved at the age of seventeen in 1962. I can remember in my early Christian days that good pastors would not address issues in the culture. They would say that we need to just focus on God and sharing the gospel. Certainly, focusing on God and sharing the gospel is vital and it must be our priority, but what they didn't see was that the enemy was using the culture to impact the church and stealing away our children and grandchildren. The enemy was so deluding and twisting our moral values that we would think as Eve did that "surely we won't die." We as Christians have been lulled to sleep while the society around us is changing drastically, and **it's time to fight back!**

In an article by Dennis Prager (April 7, 2015) titled "Americans Accelerating Decay" Dennis states several areas where America has declined. He states "that with few exceptions every aspect of American life is in decline."

- **Decline of the Family:** Nearly half of American children are born to a mother who is not married.
- **Decline of Education:** American history is being taught a lot less, and where it is taught American history is presented as the history of an immoral nation, characterized by slavery, racism, colonialism, imperialism, economic exploitation and militarism – not a country that, more than any other, has been the beacon of freedom to mankind.
- **The End of Male and Female:** Gender doesn't matter. Whether children are raised by a mother and father or two mothers or two fathers doesn't matter.

    A woman was recently kicked out of Planet Fitness for objecting to a man in a woman's locker room. She was accused of intolerance because the man said he felt like he was a woman.

- **The End of Right and Wrong:** At least two generations of American young people have been taught that moral categories are nothing more than personal (or societal) preferences.

So, clearly it is past time to fight back. John Stonestreet from Breakpoint states, "Loving our neighbors requires cultural concern, and maybe even action. There's no such thing as loving individuals without engaging the larger cultural trends that may adversely affect them."

We all need to pick a declining area and choose to fight back. I will give you some possible areas to be involved in as follows:

Pornography

Several years ago, I was traveling on business in North America. I flew into a city and rented a car to take me where I had to go. I turned on the radio. It was previously set to a station by a former driver, and I heard the most shocking statement. The person on the radio kept repeating this statement, "If you are healthy, pornography is healthy." That was the first time that I realized that some people actually believe that pornography can be good for you. How crazy is that! We have declined so drastically that now almost half of adults believe it is morally acceptable to have a sexual relationship with someone of the opposite sex to whom you are not married.

- 67% of 18-26 year old men believe viewing pornography is acceptable
- 49% of 18-26 year old women think viewing pornography is acceptable
- 42% of all adults overall

Pornography is wide spread. Craig Gross and Ron Jeremy state that "Every second, 28,258 internet users are viewing pornography. Every 39 minutes, a new pornographic video is being created in the United States. Every day, 68 million pornographic requests are searched online." They go on to say, "the porn industry has larger revenues than Microsoft, Google, Amazon, eBay, Yahoo, Apple and Netflix **combined**. In 2006, the industry had ballooned to $97.06 billion dollars." So, today it is probably much larger.

Pornography is clearly linked to violent crime. In the same article by Gross and Jermey, they state that "One of the most powerful testimonies we've ever heard regarding pornography addiction came from the serial killer Ted Bundy. This man confessed to more than 30 murders. Just before he was to be executed by electric chair on January 24, 1989, he granted an interview to James Dobson, Founder and President of the organization, Focus on the Family. **Bundy went on record to say:**

> "I've lived in prison for a long time now, and I've met a lot of men who were motivated to commit violence. Without exception, every one of them was deeply involved in pornography – deeply consumed by the addiction. The F.B.I.'s own study on serial homicide shows that the most common interest among serial killers is pornographers.
>
> I'm not blaming pornography. I'm not saying it caused me to go out and do certain things. I take full responsibility for all the things that I've done. That's not the question here. The issue is how this kind of literature contributed and helped mold and shape the kinds of violent behavior.
>
> Those of us who have been so influenced by violence in the media, particularly pornographic violence, are not some kind of inherent monsters. We are your sons and husbands. We grew up in regular families. Pornography can reach in and snatch a kid out of any house today. It snatched me out of my home 20 or 30 years ago" [iii]

More startling is that Bundy not only grew up in a regular, loving family...he grew up in a Christian home.

Dr. Mary Anne Layden stated in her report to the Kansas Legislature in 2011 that ""**I had been doing this work for more than 10 years before I realized that I had not treated one case of sexual violence that did not include pornography.**"

According to Charles Keating of Citizens for Decency Through Law, research reveals that 77 percent of child molesters of boys and 87 percent of child molesters of girls admitted imitating the sexual behavior they had seen modeled in pornography.

Sociologists Murray Straus and Larry Baron (University of New Hampshire) found that rape rates are highest in states which have high sales of sex magazines and lax enforcement of pornography laws.

We all know how pornography has spilled over into the church. According to Archdiocese of Omaha Anti-Pornography task force at the time of this publication:

- Over half of evangelical pastors admit viewing pornography
- 57% of pastors say that addiction to pornography is the most sexually damaging issue to their congregation

Child pornography is also on the rise. Approximately 20% of all internet pornography involves children. In 2003, more than 20,000 images of child pornography are posted on line every week. One hundred thousand web sites offer illegal child pornography. Not only does child porn affect the viewer but the lives of children are permanently damaged.

Maybe this could be your life's work to reduce the access to pornography by strengthen laws and generating enthusiasm to eliminate it from our culture.

Biblical Influence

In our lifetime, we have seen a dramatic change in the Bible's impact on our culture. The Bible has for the most part has been removed from public areas and the truths of scripture have little influence on society in general. The Christian historian David Barton states that the Bible was a centerpiece of our American ancestors' lives but is no longer seen as a practical guide book for society. Noah Webster who has been called the "Father of American Scholarship and Education" stated that "The Bible is the chief moral cause of all that is good and the best corrector of all that is evil in human society." The Pilgrims wanted to conform the culture to God's Word and viewed the Bible as a life manual for day to day living. Even though the Bible was the most significant book in forming our government it is now mostly confined to our churches.

Dr. Benjamin Rush in 1791 warned not to remove the Bible from public schools by stating, "In contemplating the political institutions of the United States, I lament that (if we remove the Bible from schools) we waste so much time and money in punishing crimes and take so little pains to prevent them for the Divine Book (Bible) above all others, favors that equality among mankind, that respect for just laws, and frugal virtues which constitute the soul of (our governments)"

The Bible which has been the primary source of public laws has now been removed from public view. In 1962, the Supreme Court ordered the separation of religious principles from education, and in 1963, they removed Bible reading from schools and said the Bible could damage a child psychologically. Since then, our society has gone downhill dramatically and violent crime has gone up 450 – 500 percent.

Perhaps, this could be your life goal to get the Bible back into the public arena. Maybe a goal is just to get a Bible verse in your community center or to financially support organizations that are working to publically display the Ten Commandments. People no longer fear God or man and that's why they can commit such horrific crimes.

Male and Female

God said, "Male and female He created them" but today our culture wants to strip away those differences and eliminate traditional gender roles like women giving birth to babies. Sorry just kidding. ☺ As I am writing this chapter, the latest controversy is Disney's "Beauty and the Beast." That has been called Disney's first "exclusive gay moment." Certainly, the homosexual movement has dramatically changed our culture such that a marriage is no longer viewed as solely between a man and a woman. The movement has been very successful in changing the minds of Americans such that now more than half of Americans accept homosexual relationships. Also, you no longer have to stay the way you were born. If you are a male, and want to be a female, just change. We think that God must have made some mistakes when He made us, and we can just fix it with some surgeries. You can even change daily. If you are a man and one day you think you are a woman, you can use the women's rest room. How crazy is that! Maybe this could be your life's work, to bring us back to our God given roles as men and women.

Just a couple of months, ago a man in my community Bible study testified at a county school board meeting that is contemplating the bath room change to let men use the women's room and vice versa. The board temporarily shelved the idea until the opposition quiets down.

We need to continue the battle and maybe you want to make it your fight.

Crime and Punishment

Because we have taken God out of the public arena, God is no longer feared. People can commit mass murder because they don't care if they die in the process. They don't understand that they will face their creator and that their soul lives on. In a similar way, they no longer fear man because we have so minimized punishment for crime that it not a strong deterrent and it is not exercised quickly. Our legal system takes a long time and reduces the effectiveness of punishment. Ecclesiastes 8:11, "Because the sentence against an evil deed is not executed quickly, therefore the hearts of the sons of men among them are given fully to do evil." The punishment must also fit the crime. If the punishment is not strong enough, people feel the crime is worth it. We have lost empathy for the victim and do not properly punish the criminal. Punishment is not just so that person will stop his criminal behavior but also a deterrent so that others will not commit the same crime. Deuteronomy 13:11 states, "Then all Israel will hear and be afraid, and will never again do such a wicked thing among you."

So perhaps, this could be your life's work to pursue change in our judicial system to reduce the process time and to make the punishment more appropriate for the crime.

Abortion

I know this is an issue that gets a lot of attention, but I think we need to fix it or our country will not survive. We must stop the murder of unborn babies. We are in an uproar over violent crime and how murder and violence happen so frequently. Even with as many murders that occur each year, they are still significantly lower than the number of babies killed by the abortionists. In

2015, there were slightly less than 16,000 murders in America. Abortions have been over one million per year from 1977 – 1997, and now run around 700,000 per year. Abortion murders far exceed homicides! Let's continue to reduce murders but let's also attack the abortion problem.

Maybe this could be your life's work. Get involved and work to eliminate this evil practice.

I hope these areas have given you some ideas where you can personally fight back. There are certainly other places, and maybe something else could be your area to attack. But, let's attack and with our devotion to our Lord pick up our stones and face the giant for God's glory.

You may be thinking that you are just one person and how can you make a difference? Certainly, I could give you examples from the Bible and history where God has used only one person to make a huge difference but let me give you another idea.

The financial resources and purchasing power of older adults will become the largest spending group in about ten years. Businesses are starting to recognize this and are targeting seniors to get their dollars. They are working on products specifically for older consumers. Matthew Boyle states that "The world has never before seen such a powerful market with about 3 trillion dollars to spend in the U.S. alone. In 2017, almost half of the U.S. population will be 50 and older. They will control a full 70% of the disposable income, according to Nielsen. By 2050, there will be 161 million 50 and older consumers, a 63% increase over 2010.

This huge financial army could virtually change the world!!!

How and where we spend our money can have a tremendous moral impact on our culture. Just recently a boycott of Target changed their bathroom policy. We can certainly individually make moral decisions in where we shop and buy but if organized we could again change the world. We should not support companies that support immoral activities or organizations. We should financially support organizations that are in the battle.

John Stonestreet in a Breakpoint article states, "Loving our neighbors requires concern, analysis, and maybe even action. There's no such thing as loving individuals without engaging the larger cultural trends that may adversely affect them."

Again, it's time to fight back!

John MacArthur states that "Many believers are inclined to accommodate every worldly practice. Under the pretense of relevance, they copy the world's materialistic and immoral ways. When the world becomes preoccupied with material things, so has the church. When the world lowers its sexual standards, so has the church. When the world becomes entertainment crazed, so has the church. When the world glorifies self-worth and self-fulfillment, so has the church. "

Daniel 11:32b "but the people who know their God will display strength and take action."

So, we need to take the battle to the world, and also develop close mentoring relationships with those younger to help them in the battle.

ARE WE HELPING THE YOUNGER?

Chapter 16
By Personal Relationships

Job 12:12 "Wisdom is with aged men, *with* long life is understanding."

Experience is a big deal

Agatha Christy, "The young people think the old people are fools -- but the old people know the young people are fools."

I worked my way through college by going to the University of Cincinnati in their co-op engineering program. I would work for 3 ½ months and then attend school for 2 ½ months. It was a difficult five year program. At the beginning, we started with 150 electrical engineering students and of those 150 about 45 graduated. Needless to say at graduation I was relieved and excited. At the time of my graduation in 1968, I had an old Mercury Comet for a car and thought I should reward myself with a new one. I had accepted a job at IBM but had no money left, only school debt. Actually, when I received my first IBM check, the only money we had was the change in my pocket. But, I thought I/we needed a new car before we traveled all the way from Cincinnati, Ohio to Endwell, New York. So, I went to a local car dealer and fell in love with a 1967 red Dodge Dart with bucket seats and a floor gear shift. It looked great, and I was smitten. I thought I deserved a new car for my hard work so I proceeded to buy it. I paid the sticker price, and they gave me a loan with no down payment and a payoff schedule. The only problem was that the first payment was due before I would receive my first IBM check. When I told the dealership about the problem they said just to forget the first payment, start with the second and just pay 35 payments not all 36. That should have been a clue that I was making a bad deal, but I was young and inexperienced. Actually after buying the car, I went home and found the same car from that dealer advertised in the paper for less money than what I paid. No wonder they could drop the first payment. I learned a life- long lesson and discovered that experience is a big deal.

Your life experiences are valuable and can be a great help to someone with less experience. How often have we seen someone making a bad decision and knew they would pay dearly for it later? Often we don't have a close enough relationship with them to give advice, or perhaps they just don't want it. When we are rejected in trying to give advice we generalize and think all younger people don't want advice. That's just not the case.

Young people need and want advice

In a UK study about social welfare issues they found that young people's access to advice was disturbingly poor. They want advice but only from people whom they trust. Getting that trusted advice makes a big positive difference to the outcome of their problems. Even though this study is about social issues, I think some of it can apply to personal issues as well. The younger generations want advice but only from people they trust. So, we must develop relationships with them to gain their trust and then tell them our story.

Joel 1:3 states "Tell your sons about it, and *let* your sons *tell* their sons, and their sons the next generation."

John MacArthur says "The pedagogical importance of reciting the Lord's mighty works to subsequent generations is heavily underscored by this three-fold injunction."

Tell your story

As we develop relationships, we must tell our story and how we learned about the goodness of God through our own life. A good way to start is to think how God has impacted your life at different points. Deuteronomy 32:7 states, "Remember the days of old, consider the years of all generations. Ask your father, and he will inform you, your elders, and they will tell you." John MacArthur says this means that "this is a call to reflect on past history and to inquire about the lessons to be learned."

It could be from a time before or after you became a believer but tell your story. Here are some highlights from my life at different stages:

- **10 years old**

I was the oldest grandchild on my mother's side of the family. Her parents had a hard life while their kids were still in the home. My grandfather was an alcoholic and often hit my grandmother. After their kids were out of the home, she decided she suffered enough and said she was moving out. This statement was devastating to my grandfather, and he decided to get help through AA. He got sober and never went back to drinking. So their years together after their kids left home were their best, and I received the benefit of that. They would take me on vacations and trips, as well as on occasion, stays in their home. I was sort of the only child they raised together. My grandmother was the most significant godly influence on me in those early years. She taught me the importance of prayer. Their retirement years were their best and my grandmother said the secret to life was to "keep Looking Up." That has stuck with me to this day and it is my constant advice to my grandchildren.

- **20 years old**

At twenty years of age, I was in college and married with a child. During my third year of a five year program, I brought Carol and Renee with me during my school quarter. School was always intense, and I didn't realize that we were running out of money and still had about two weeks to go before my work session. That's back when we didn't have credit cards, and when you ran out of money you ran out. I knew I could contact someone back home for help. However, about the same time I realized we were out of money, we got money in the mail from my grandmother and Carol's aunt on the same day. This was the only time we received money in the mail, and they both said they just felt we needed it even though we had not said anything. It was my first significant experience of God's provision, and it has stuck with me to this day.

- **30 years old**

At around thirty years of age, I can remember two significant events that God used in my life. The first was my mother's battle with cancer. She contracted ovarian cancer. It was not operable, and the chemo didn't work. Her battle was probably the most significant event (outside of my salvation) in my life that God used to grow me spiritually. It was the first time I witnessed to anyone and the first time I prayed in public. My mother would just say, "Ronnie let's pray" no matter who was in the room. This time certainly increased my prayer life, and we would travel back often from Virginia to Pennsylvania to see her. She seemed to hold on until God impressed on me that she was not going to recover from this disease. While in Virginia one morning, I prayed that if she couldn't recover that God would take her so she wouldn't suffer. As near as I can tell, she took a turn for the worse that day and died within 24 hours. I learned for the first time the importance of praying in God's will.

Just before that time, I learned that God truly answers prayer. We were living in New York, and I received an offer from IBM to move to Virginia. I didn't want to move as we had just bought a home and were finally getting settled. Through my seeking God about the decision, He clearly impressed on me that we should move. We did, and now as we look back we can see the reasons why.

- **40 years old**

Around the age of 40, we were attending Faith Bible Church. I was on the elder board. Being involved in church leadership, I got to experience spiritual warfare firsthand. The enemy wants to divide us in both the church and our families. I also experienced the awesome privilege of developing close relationships with missionaries. Their commitment in serving our Lord made a great impact on me personally. My wife, Carol worked for a new mission agency that started in our church and is now known as Pioneers. It was a great time of spiritual growth for me, and I had the privilege of leading my first person to Christ at this time.

- **50 years old**

The year before I turned 50 years old, my grandmother on my mother's side (Alma Catt) died at the age of 97. As I said before, she was my strongest godly influence in my younger years. At the time of her death, both my kids were married, and we had three grandchildren. At her funeral, it was customary for each family to have a private session to say their good-bye's. My thought was that this didn't make any sense since she was no longer there. It was just the body she used for 97 years and had now abandoned. So, I took my family up beside the coffin and just started to pray. It was a strange feeling as though I wasn't speaking but the words kept coming out. I prayed about her life, the example she left for us, her salvation, and that she was no longer here but in heaven. The words kept coming. After I finished, I opened my eyes to find most all of the rest of the family had crowded around to hear. My uncles, their families, my siblings, cousins, etc. were all right there. As I reflect back at that time, it was like an Elijah/Elisha moment. It was as though God was passing the spiritual leadership from her to me, and I was to be the spiritual leader of my extended family. I hope with the Lord's help I have upheld my responsibility.

60 years old

At around 60 years old, actually 58, I was fired from my staff job at Reston Bible Church. To this day, that has been the greatest surprise in my life. I had quit my IBM/Lockheed Martin engineering job at 55 years old and accepted my dream job as Executive Pastor at RBC. At the time of being hired, I was an elder at RBC. They wanted me to be on staff and manage the church operation of about 1,200 people. I loved my job and enjoyed going to work every day and it was going great. We started a building campaign and purchased some land. Everyone was excited and giving sacrificially. Then, I got fired. I had planned to work there until I was 70 but God had other plans. I now think that God was behind the firing. We had to sell our house to survive while I looked for work. I eventually got a part time job with a small engineering company, and we moved into a 55 and older community. As a result of the changes, I wrote my first book on evangelism, and I started to teach and preach. Without that change, I would have never had the courage to perform my grandson's wedding or my brother's funeral. God has been so good. I'll tell you more of the story at age 70.

- **70 years old**

At around 70 years old, actually 71, God halted the financial games of keeping all the balls in the air. Over the twelve years after leaving RBC, God provided part time jobs for me and Carol to keep us afloat. Last year, He stopped all that by selling our house and giving us a condo in the same community mortgage free. We now have more income than expenses and are without the need to work for the first time in our lives. We now are truly retired and can devote more time to serve God in whatever ways He wants us to do that. He has even provided time to finish this book which I hope has been an encouragement to you to finish strong and to "Soar into Heaven." The house sale and condo purchase were absolutely perfect. Our house sold in three weeks to a wonderful Christian couple and for the exact amount we needed to be able to purchase the new condo mortgage free. We closed on the sale of our house on May 18th, purchased the condo on May 19th, and moved in on May 20th. The condo was new and under construction. They weren't sure when it would be finished, but it was finished when we needed it and the move went great! This reminded me of the money in the mail at age 20 and again confirmed for me that God is our provider.

Please take some time now and remember how God has blessed you at various ages so you can be ready to encourage those who are younger and going through some of the same things that you have already experienced.

Deuteronomy 11: 19 "You shall teach them to your sons, talking of them when you sit in your house and when you walk along the road and when you lie down and when you rise up."

Build Relationships

Look for opportunities in your community or your church to build relationships with younger people. They will appreciate it, and you will both be blessed by it. Several years ago when we first started attending Reston Bible Church, we were looking for a small group, and Carol heard a woman say they needed an older couple in their group. Well, we were now an older couple and needed a group so we joined. After being in the group for some time, it grew and needed to split. We agreed to lead half of the group. We didn't know if any of the younger couples would want to come with us, but they did and it was a great time for all of us. We have all gone our separate ways, but we all look back at that time as precious in our lives.

Grandparenting

A few years ago, a good friend of mine, Dave Duffy, died of pancreatic cancer. I attended his memorial service and listened as most of his grandchildren told how he had impacted their lives. I wanted to have the same kind of impact with my family. I hadn't done a very good job of telling my children how God had worked in my life, so I wanted to do a better job with my grandchildren. I had heard of someone who would periodically tell their family how God was working in their life, and I determined to do the same. So, I started a weekly email called "Papa Weekly." I have been doing it now for about five years. I don't always do it every week and lately have missed a lot, but I just try to tell them what I have learned or what God is presently doing. I have randomly picked some and included them here as an encouragement to you, that perhaps you could do the same.

Papa Weekly (June 6, 2012)

Yesterday, we went to a funeral of a longtime friend (Dave Duffy). It was a great service, and I was again reminded of the shortness of this life. It seems like it was just yesterday that I broke my hand in middle school, tried to give a speech in my History class in High school, or pulled a prank during senior week in college. James 4:14b says, "You are just a vapor that appears for a little while and then vanishes away." Our life is short compared to eternity, whether we live to 20, 40, 60 or 80. It's still short. So, use the time that God gives you wisely.

  Keep Looking Up,

   Love,

   Dad/Papa

PS I will attempt to send you a note weekly about things that God has taught me the past week – hope it helps

Papa Weekly (August 29, 2012)

God hears our prayers! What great news. The great God of creation hears our prayers. He is interested in the small details of our lives and will respond.

In II Kings 19:20 & 20:5, God tells the king, Hezekiah, that He heard his prayer and God also responded by saving them from Assyria and agreed to extend his life. So if we truly believed that God hears our prayers, we would pray more. So, pray more and see what God will do.

  Keep looking up,

   Love

   Dad/Papa

Papa Weekly (June 12, 2013)

We live in a time where everyone is out for themselves. The common question today is "What's in it for me?" If someone does something unselfishly for someone else it shows up on the

evening news. How sad is that. ☐ Phil 2:3 states, "Do nothing from selfishness or empty conceit, but with humility of mind regard one another as more important than yourselves." This doesn't say do something unselfishly but **EVERYTHING!** I don't know about you but it is hard for me to do things unselfishly. But, God commands it. Actually this is the key to any successful relationship, especially a marriage. So do something today completely unselfishly and,
  Keep Looking Up,
   Love,
   Dad/Papa

Papa Weekly (April 4, 2014)

How should we respond to people who mistreat us? Should we pay back, eye for an eye etc. What does God say?? Rom 12:14, "Bless those who persecute you, bless and do not curse." 12:17, Never pay back evil for evil to anyone. 12:18, If possible, so far as it depends on you, be at peace with all men. 12:21. Do not be overcome with evil, but overcome evil with good. So be good &
  Keep Looking Up,
   Love,
   Dad/Papa

Papa Weekly (October 1, 2014)

Tuesday this week, we discussed Phil 2:12 which states that "you must work out your own salvation." So, what does that mean? It certainly doesn't mean that we must work for our salvation. Eph. 2:8, 9 states, "For by grace are you saved through faith, yet not of yourselves, it is a gift of God, not by works lest anyone should boast." But it does mean if we have truly given our life to Christ it will show in what we do and who we are. If someone says they have trusted Christ as their Savior but they don't want to pray, read their Bible, or be in Christian community then they probably

aren't saved. As someone once said, they are professors and not possessors. **We do what we believe**. So, be doers of the word and not just hearers &
  Keep Looking Up,
    Love,
  Dad/Papa

Papa Weekly (July 8, 2015)

Our society wonders why we have church and school shootings and other such crimes. The main reason is that we have taken God out of the culture. The psalmist in Psalm 10:6 states, the wicked…. All his thoughts are "There is no God" or he says in verse 11 "God has forgotten; He has hidden His face, He will never see it." If the attacker believes he will answer to God he will not be as quick to murder etc. So, let's put God back into our lives wherever we can &
  Keep Looking Up,
    Love,
  Dad/Papa

Papa Weekly (September 16, 2016)

Did you know that there are now estimated to be 100,000,000,000,000,000,000,000,000,000 stars? (100 octillion) But because of all that is required for complex life forms to exist (about 20 major factors) that a lot of people believe it is mathematically impossible for another earth to exist. How awesome is that! God has so uniquely created this earth that it might be the only one of its kind in the universe! In Romans 1:20, Paul states that because of this unique creation "man is without excuse." God has so reveled Himself in creation such that man needs nothing else to understand that there must be a creator behind it. So when you talk to others about God, talk about this great creation that shouts the glory of God. And
  Keep Looking Up,

Love,
Dad/Papa

Please take time to build relationships with younger people. Tell your story, both how God has worked over the years and how He is working today. I think this verse should be our theme to motivate us to action.

Deuteronomy 32:7 "Remember the days of old; consider the generations past. Ask your father and he will tell you, your elders, and they will explain it to you."

Psalm 71:18 (ESV) "So even to old age and gray hairs, O God, do not forsake me, until I proclaim Your might to another generation, Your power to all those to come."

RISE UP! RISE UP!

Chapter 17
Conclusion

Ephesians 5:14b "Awake, sleeper, and arise from the dead, and Christ will shine on you."

We all want to make our life count and to have God say well done when we get to heaven, but the first step is getting to heaven. I have addressed this book to Christian Senior Adults. By that I mean those of our age bracket who have put their faith and trust in Jesus Christ as their personal Savior. If you have never taken this step, I urge you to do so now as we discussed life is short and there is no guarantee for tomorrow.

So, for the time we have left on this earth how can we be effective in God's army? Remember we are extremely valuable to God. He can use us greatly if we commit to give this time of our lives totally to Him and not to ourselves. **We need to rise up!!**

Again Fight Back

My fear is that we are so much engrained into the culture that the immorality we see no longer bothers us. It's like the frog in the pot of water on the stove that keeps getting hotter and hotter, but he doesn't notice it until he dies in a pot of boiling water. God told the angel to spare the men of Israel who were still upset about the culture. In Ezekiel 9:4, God said to the angel, "Go through the midst of the city, *even* through the midst of Jerusalem, and put a mark on the foreheads of the men who sigh and groan over all the abominations which are being committed in its midst." Then, God told the angel to strike everyone who no longer is upset about the immorality in the culture. Don't be unmarked but marked and commit to make an impact on the culture while we have time.

Psalms 97:10a "Hate evil, you who love the Lord,"

I Corinthians 5:2 "You have become arrogant and have not mourned instead, so that the one who had done this deed would be removed from your midst."

Be a watchman

Ezekiel was appointed a watchman for the nation of Israel. Ezekiel 33:7 states, "Now as for you, son of man, I have appointed you a watchman for the house of Israel; so you will hear a message from My mouth and give them warning from Me." God established him to warn Israel just as a watchman will warn of an incoming attack. I think God has appointed us as watchmen for America. We can see the oncoming disaster. We must be diligent to warn unbelievers and believers alike to turn to God and serve Him gladly while we can, and perhaps the heart of America will turn to God and He will bless us again.

Hosea 4:1, 2 "Listen to the word of the LORD, O sons of Israel, for the LORD has a case against the inhabitants of the land, because there is no faithfulness or kindness or knowledge of God in the land. *There is* swearing, deception, murder, stealing and adultery. They employ violence, so that bloodshed follows bloodshed."

Be a shepherd

Be a good shepherd and feed the flock. Hear the word of the Lord, teach it to others, and shepherd the flock. Don't be like the shepherds in Ezekiel's time who only fed themselves but study hard and feed others.

Ezekiel 34:8b "but rather the shepherds fed themselves and did not feed My flock."

Determine to hang tough

Continue to pray and live righteously because your prayer's effectiveness is somewhat dependent on your righteousness. Ezekiel 14:20, "even *though* Noah, Daniel and Job were in its midst, as I live," declares the Lord GOD, "they could not deliver either *their* son or *their* daughter. They would deliver only themselves by their righteousness." This is one of the few places in the Bible where God indicates that a person's righteousness will have some impact on God's judgement over a nation. Israel was so wicked that Noah, Daniel , and Job could have only saved themselves.

We are truly the preservative for our society. Mark 9:50 states, "Salt is good; but if the salt becomes unsalty, with what will you make it salty *again*? Have salt in yourselves, and be at peace with one another." John MacArthur states, "Salt was an essential item in first-century Palestine. In a hot climate, without refrigeration, salt was the practical way of preserving food. The work of the Word and the Spirit produce godly character, enabling a person to act as a preservative in society." So, stay salty, it's vital to our future as a country.

In Charles Swindol's book "Living above the Level of Mediocrity" he states that we must determine to hang tough. Not to give in or give up but keep on keeping on. Chuck states that there is no secret formula like some miracle cure-all but with the Lord's help exercise the sheer determination not to fall and to live above the level of mediocrity.

Amy Hanson states, "It's no shock that the culture tries to lure us into believing that the last 30 years of life are about focusing on ourselves. However, the Bible speaks in contrast to this mindset and reminds us that we are to have an eternal focus. Paul's exhortation in Colossians 3:2 is that we are to set our minds on things above, not on earthly things."

Caution

Most of the book talks about the importance of our continuing to grow in the wisdom and knowledge of the Lord. Experience is a big deal but it is not a guarantee of wisdom. Job 32:9 states, "The abundant *in years* may not be wise, nor may elders understand justice."

The culture wants us to focus on ourselves during this time. We are supposed to create a bucket list and then go do it. We should buy an RV, travel or move to Florida etc. Although there is nothing specifically wrong with those things, they can lead to problems if we do them for ourselves not because we want to serve God better. On one of our trips back from a week in Florida, I stopped to get gas. Across from me was an RV also coming back from Florida and I noticed the license plate "TIME 4 US." How appropriate. It says the previous part of their lives was for other people, and now at this time their focus was on themselves. Please don't do the same. **Make a bucket list about serving God and then go do it.**

Senior Christian adults are truly a resource and not a ministry. Sure we can have ministries to senior adults and that is great. But, we should view ourselves as a resource, first to God, and then to our church, family, and society. If you and your church could catch this vison, we could turn the world upside down for God. As I have said and truly believe, **the future of the church in America lies with the older not the younger.**

Again, I think Senior Christian Adults are the greatest untapped resource in modern America today. We are totally clueless about what God can and wants to do through us. Please, after you put this book down make your bucket list for God. Then be committed to follow through. Hang tough even though our body is failing. Continue to grow spiritually, and **SOAR INTO HEAVEN** at full speed!

Isaiah 46:4 "Even to *your* old age I will be the same, and even to *your* graying years I will bear *you*! I have done *it*, and I will carry *you*; and I will bear *you* and I will deliver *you*."

Psalm 145:4 "One generation shall praise Your works to another, and shall declare Your mighty acts."

2 Timothy 4:7-8 "I have fought the good fight, I have finished the course, I have kept the faith; in the future there is laid up for me the crown of righteousness, which the Lord, the righteous Judge, will award to me on that day; and not only to me, but also to all who have loved His appearing."

Hebrews 3:13-14 "But encourage one another day after day, as long as it is *still* called "Today," so that none of you will be hardened by the deceitfulness of sin. For we have become partakers of Christ, if we hold fast the beginning of our assurance firm until the end,"

Psalm 92:12-15 "The righteous man (or woman) will flourish like the palm tree, he will grow like a cedar in Lebanon. Planted in the house of the Lord, they will flourish in the courts of our God. They will still yield fruit in old age; they shall be full of sap and very green. To declare that the Lord is upright; He is my rock, and there is no unrighteousness in Him."

If after reading this you have other ideas or comments, please contact me. My email is ronbowen07@comcast.net. Also, if possible, I would love to speak to your senior group. So, continue the fight and

   Keep Looking Up,
   Ron

Bibliography

Chapter 1

Jacobs, Debra Forbes quoted Donna Ballman November 3, 2013
Satron, Richard, Staff Writer U.S. News and World Report, October 8, 2013, Boomers forced to retire face unexpected challenges
Fitch, Victoria, The Psychologist Tasks of Old Age 1988
Howard, Victoria, Aging in Enlightened Society 2015
Wilson, Des, Daily Mail, May 17, 2014, www.dailymail.co.uk/news/article - 263,251
Callahan, Daniel, New York Times, On Dying After Your Time, November 30, 2013
McCurry Justin, The Guardian, Let elderly people 'hurry up and die', says Japanese minister,
    January 27, 2013
Lewis, Ed, CE National (Church Effectiveness) Keep older adults in church
American Psychological Association web site, www.APA.org/Pi/Aging/Resources/Guides/Older
    Older Adults' Health and Age-related Changes
        Changes in mental health and mental processes
        Physical changes

Chapter 2

Reade, Nathaniel, AARP the Magazine, The Surprising Truth About Older Workers, August 2013
Brindle, The Guardian, Older people are an asset, not a drain, March 1, 2011
Martin, Jen, Corporation for National and Community Service, Health Benefits of Volunteering

for older Americans, Contributions of Older Volunteers Honored this Week, AARP May 8, 2012

Anderson, Jeff, Why Grandparents Matter More than Ever, October 23, 2013

American Psychological Association web site, www.APA.org/Pi/Aging/Resources/Guides/Older

Roland, Thomas W., *The Athletic Clock*, Human Kinetics – Excerpts, 2011

Edelman, Bob, Older Workers Are America's Most Valuable Assets!, November 9, 2014

Chapter 3

US Social Security Administration Quote from Aging in the United States – The Christian Response, The United Methodist Church 2012, The Book of Resolution of the United Methosidst Church

Bendavid, Naftali, The Wall Street Journal, Europe's Empty Churches Go On Sale, 2015

Contreaas M.D., Francisco, Look Younger Love Longer, page 155, Dr. Grossarth –Matrick Statement

Chapter 4

Bridges, Jerry, *The Fruitful Life*, Nav Press 2006

Bearing Fruit, National Council for the Elderly, 1993

Levy and Slade, Longevity Increased by Positive Self-perceptions of Aging, apa.org/pubs/journals/releases/psp-832261.

Chapter 5

The Encyclopedia of Aging and the Elderly Anxiety (stress)

www.medrounds.org/encyclopedia-of-aging/2005/12/anxiety-stress.html

Arrest for allegedly pepper spraying a disabled woman (Herald Net) July 30, 2012

Heraldnet.com/news/arrest-for-alleged-pepper-spraying-a-disabled-woman/

Elderly woman crossing the street (You Tube) www.youtubecom/watch?v=u2z6r-6g11v

Chapter 6

Cohen, Ben, Why Wanting to be Rich is a Form of Mental Illness, April 12, 2012,

www.huffingtonpost.com/ben-cohen/why-wanting-to-be-rich-is-b-1419776.html

The Necessity of Wealth, President Andrews of Brown University, June 25, 1893

Most Americans Do Not Have a Strong Desire to be Rich, Gallup, December 11, 2006

Blackman, Andrew, Can Money Bring you Happiness, The Wall Street Journal,

November 10, 2014

Gilbert, Dwayne, The Desire to be Rich,

www.selfgrowth.com/articles/The-Desire-to-be-rich.html

Justice, Richard, Gibbs Now Open About Laws in His Life, Washington Post Staff Writer,

February 1, 1991

Walsh, Colleen Money Spent on Others Can Bring Happiness, Harvard Gazette, April 17, 2008

(Prof. Dunn, page 55)

French, Katy, Ben Franklin's advice to pay it forward, Visual News, January 14, 2016

Hammond, Lily Hardy, In the Garden of Delight, 1916, Thomas Y, Crowell Company, New York

New World Encyclopedia, John D. Rockefeller quote,

www.newworldencyclopedia.org/John-D-Rockefeller

United States Department of Agricultural (USDA), Economic Research Service – 2015,
August 17 2016, www.ers.usda.gov
Pope, Global Rich List – 2017, www.globalrichlist.com/#NA, September 9, 2017
Carmichal, Amy, quote, Good Reads,
www.goodreads.com/author/quotes/3935881.Amy-Carmichal
Pay it forward United Kingdom, Ralph Waldo Emerson quote, July 16, 2013
www.payitforwarduk.net/blog/ralph-waldo-emerson

Chapter 7

Colson, Chuck, Can We be Good Without God?, posted April 26, 2003
townhall.com/columinist/chuckcolson/2003/04/26/can-we-be-good-without-god-n986680
Warren, Rick, 7 Ways God Will Evaluate Your Faithfulness, September 12, 2013,
pastors.com community pastors.com/7-ways-god-will-evaluate-faithfulness/
Sussman, Dalia, Who Goes to Church? ABC News, March 1,
abcnews.go.com/US/story?id=90372&page1
Suicide Facts and Statistics, 2015, American Foundation for Suicide Prevention
afsp.org/about-suicide-statistics
Koening, Don, The Death of Integrity in American, 2008
thepropheticyears.com/comments/The-Death-of-Integrity-in-America.html
Evans, Martin, Honesty Test: lack of integrity is bad for the economy, scientists conclude, January 2012, integrity study by Essex University
Epperson, Sharon, Retiring abroad? Check out these IRA strategies, May 6, 2014

Cnbc.com/2014/05/06/retiring-abroad-check-out-these-ira-strategies.html

Chapter 8

Barna Survey, April 28, 2013, The Traits That Make a Leader, barna.org/culture-articles/609-what-do-americans-really-think-about-the-bible

Konkola, Kari, Have We Lost Humility? Journal from National Humanities Institute, Cma-ministry.org/Studies/Konkola%20have%20we%20lost%20humility.pdf

Christian Bible Reference Site, Humility, November 10, 2015, christianbiblereference.org/humility.htm, website by Cliff and Helen Leitch

Plantinga, Harry, St. Augustine of Hippo quote, Sin of Pride, Christian Classics Ethereal Library Ccel.org/ccel.schaff/npaf105.xii.xxxvii.html

Burton, Nell, Is Pride a Virtue or a Vice? April 24, 2012, psychologytoday.com/blog/hide-and-seek/201204/is-pride-virtue-or-vice.

Ministries of Senior Adults in Christ, May 26, 2013, What does the Bible say about Pride?

Chapter 9

Pfan, Wade, Three Questions to Evaluate Longevity Risk for Retirees, August 23, 2016, Society of Actuaries, forbes.com/site/wadepfan/2016/08/23/three-questions-to-evaluate-longevity-risk-for-retiree/2/#55e3297d27b4

Krantz-Kent, Rachel and Stewart, Jay, How do older Americans spend their time? May 2007,

Monthly Labor Review, bls.gov/opub/min/2007/05/art2ful.pdf
Stanley, Andy, DVD – Time

Chapter 10

Deaton, Todd, Prayer: No. 1 issue in churches, survey of leaders shows, The Courier (Baptist Courier), March 7, 2006, 2005 Life Way Christian Resoquoteurces survey

Brooks, Carol, What Really Caused the Downward Spiral? www.implainsite.org/what-happened-when-the-praying.html

Miller, J.R., The Sweet Fragrance of Prayer, 1888, (N.D.) Retrieved December 14, 2005 www.gracegems.org/Miller/sweet-fragrance-of-prayer.html

Bounds, E.M. quote "Praying is the most important thing on earth." Paul, the Teacher of Prayer

Bounds, E.M. *The Classic collection on Prayer,* Bridge-Logos, Orlando, FL 2001, Edited by Harold Chadwick

Chapter 11

Nordstrom, Nancy Mery. Top 10 Benefits of Lifelong Learning, July 28, 2008, SelfGrowth.com

The State of the Bible: Six Trends for 2014, barna.org/barna-update/culture/664-the-state-of-the-bible-6-trends-for-2014

U.S. Religious Knowledge Survey, September 28, 2010, Pew Research Center Pweforum.org/2010/09/28/u-s-religious-knowledge-survey

Chapter 12

Warren, Rick, God Calls You to Serve Others, May 21, 2014

Graham, Billy quote, GOODREADS,
www.goodreads.com/quotes/7237162-the-highest-form-of-worship-is-the-worship-of-unselfish

Greater Goodness post,
http://goodness.greatergood.com/up-content/uploads/2015/09/ageless service.jpg

Hanson, Amy, Creating New Opportunities for Older Adults to Serve, 2007, Leadership Network
http://www.leadnet.org

Thomas, Bill, Dr Bill Thomas experiment, 2015, Washington Post

Peach, David, Putting Others Before Yourself: 7 Great Tips, February 4, 2013,
http://www.what Christianswanttoknow.com/putting-others-before-yourself-7-great-tips, printed February 10, 2010

Volunteering and its Surprising Benefits Help Guide

Chapter 13

Aldrich, Joseph C. *Life-style Evangelism: Crossing Traditional Boundaries to Reach the*
Unbelieving World. Portland, OR: Multnomah, 1981. Print.

"The Barna Group - 20 Years of Surveys Show Key Differences in the Faith of America's Men and
Women." *The Barna Group - 20 Years of Surveys Show Key Differences in the Faith of*
America's Men and Women. N.p., n.d. Web. 13 July 2012.

"The Barna Group - A New Generation Expresses Its Skepticism and Frustration with
Christianity." *The Barna Group - A New Generation Expresses Its Skepticism and*
Frustration with Christianity. N.p., n.d. Web. 18 May 2012.

"The Barna Group - Americans Identify Their Most Important Relationships." *The Barna Group –*
Americans Identify Their Most Important Relationships. N.p., n.d. Web. 20 Dec. 2011.

"The Family under Attack." *Legatus Magazine RSS*. N.p., n.d. Web. 28 Jan. 2013.
Hybels, Bill, and Mark Mittelberg. *Becoming a Contagious Christian*. Grand Rapids, MI:
    Zondervan Pub. House, 1994. Print.
"John MacArthur Study Bible." *John MacArthur Study Bible*. N.p., n.d. Web. 28 Jan. 2013.
"The Last Days." *The Decline Of Christianity In America*. N.p., n.d. Web. 12 Mar. 2012.
Lucado, Max, and David Drury. *Out Live Your Life: Participant's Guide*. Nashville, TN: Thomas
    Nelson, 2010. Print.
Mittelberg, Mark, Lee Strobel, and Bill Hybels. *Becoming a Contagious Christian:*
    Communicating Your Faith in a Style That Fits You : Participant's Guide. Grand Rapids,
    MI: Zondervan Pub. House, 1995. Print.
Poole, Garry. *Seeker Small Groups: Engaging Spiritual Seekers in Life-changing Discussions*.
    Grand Rapids, MI: Zondervan, 2003. Print.

Chapter 14

Wilke, Jay and Sand, Lydia, Older Americans' Moral Attitudes Changing
Gallups' 2013, Values and Beliefs poll, May 207, 2013
MacArthur, John, Following Godly Examples, July 16, 1989

Chapter 15

Prager, Dennis, American's Accelerating Decay, April 7, 2015
Stonestreet, John, Breakpoint, "Should Christians Engage the Culture?" August 1, 2016
Pornography Statistics, Anti-Pornography Task Force, Archdiocese of Omaha, http://archkck.org

Gross, Craig and Jeremy Ron, Sound off in The Great Porn Debate, Risen Magazine

Biggs, Abigail, Dr. May Anne Layden quote, Pornography and Crime, July 21, 2016

Rogers, Jay, Director, The Documented Effects of Pornography the Forerunner, November 1,
    1991, Murray Stauss, Charles Keating quotes

Boyle, Matthew, Aging Boomers Stump Marketers Eyeing $15 Trillion Prize, September 17, 2013

Chapter 16

Kenrick, James, Young people's access to advice, October 2009

Chapter 17

Hanson, Amy, Baby Boomer Ministry, January 8, 2016

Acknowledgments

I am grateful to all who have guided, participated, encouraged, and prayed for the completion of this book. The second time around was not less work but at least I was aware of the process. Thank you to our senior adult community group (ENCORE!) at McLean Bible Church. They encouraged me and allowed me to teach each chapter to them as I completed it.

Thank you to my reviewers; Bob Bantle and Ken Weinzapfel. Thank you Harry Soderberg who gave me the idea for the title. Also, a thank you to Paul Montgomery who gave me the idea for the cover and to my grandson Zac Bowen who did the final design.

A special thank you to my wife Carol for her support by allowing me to work on it for over about a four year period

Finally, I am truly grateful to my Lord and Savior Jesus Christ, for saving me and allowing me to serve Him in this way. God is truly at work, and I am living a dream.

Made in the USA
Middletown, DE
12 May 2019